'Engaging and beautifully written . . . Gaw's nature writing scintillates'
– *The Countryman*

'Gaw is an excellent writer . . . [his] spirited book will encourage others to seek out such waterways, and to appreciate the importance of conserving them'
– Nancy Campbell, *Times Literary Supplement*

'It's just glorious . . . a marvellous book . . . it really put me in a good mood'
– Georgey Spanswick, BBC Radio

'Seen from the water, Britain's familiar landscapes are made mesmerisingly new. *The Pull of the River* is a hugely satisfying work of exploration and reclamation, and one that will have you itching to cast off on your own riparian adventure'
– Melissa Harrison, author of *Rain: Four Walks in English Weather*

'Following in the long and distinguished tradition of *The Wind in the Willows* and *Three Men in a Boat*, Matt Gaw spends his time 'messing about in boats'. In doing so, he entertains not only himself but us, in this delightful account of exploring the wonder of our waterways'
– Stephen Moss, author and naturalist

'A Lark for the soul'
– Paul Evans, author of *Field Notes from the Edge*

THE PULL OF
THE RIVER

THE PULL OF THE RIVER

A journey into
the wild and
watery heart
of Britain

MATT GAW

Elliott&Thompson

First published 2018 by
Elliott and Thompson Limited
27 John Street
London WC1N 2BX
www.eandtbooks.com

This paperback edition first published in 2019

ISBN: 978-1-78396-435-2

9 8 7 6 5 4 3 2 1

A catalogue record for this book is available from the British Library.

Typesetting: Marie Doherty
Printed in the UK by CPI Group (UK) Ltd, Croydon, CR0 4YY

For Jen, Seth and Eliza

Contents

      The Severn

10.   Into the wild   231
      The Great Glen Trail

      Acknowledgements   259

      Index   261

      About the author   270

Prologue

This is just a wet run, a jaunt to celebrate the building of the canoe, but I'm already lost to the water: the way she holds us, the gentle current squeezing us downstream like muscles inside the throat of some giant snake. The river here is wide and soft, bobbled and furred with a yellow fuzz of catkins blown from groups of willow that lower their tresses to the water like women washing their hair. We are moving slowly, each paddle stroke sending up tiny green whirlpools that dance and wink in the summer evening's light. Behind us we leave a wobbling trail of water, folding in on itself and disappearing with just the smallest of bow waves that shiver to the muddy bank.

The pair of us — my friend James Treadaway and I — set out just under an hour ago from Sudbury Water Meadows, humping the Canadian canoe past the last of the picnickers and the first of the cider drinkers. We heaved her into position and slid her nose-first into the water, wincing at the sound of her wooden hull scraping along the platform and sighing with relief when she didn't sink to the river's silty bottom. It was

James who built this canoe. A suburban Noah, he beavered away in his garden while his bemused neighbours peered over the fence, offering encouragement and the odd glass of orange squash. Like me, he has little experience of being on the water, but said he felt compelled to make a boat; spending months bending, shaping and gluing wood, before painting the canoe's handsome curves and broad bottom a joyous nautical red – the colour of Mae West's lips.

The canoe is high in the water and reassuringly stable, but it took until the frothing flow of Cornard Weir for us to learn how to keep her steady, our rookie strokes pulling and pushing the canoe's nose from bank to bank like a swinging compass needle. Once, twice, three times we ploughed at speed into the side or plunged through thrashing branches and into reeds, emerging sheepish and covered with downy seeds and a boat-load of surprised insects. The rhythm is easy now, the lifting and the pulling of the paddles unthinking and unhurried, minds and boat adrift.

In front of me James gestures with his hand. He doesn't need to say anything. Both of us have grown up near this river. Played on its banks, shinned up its trees and cooled off in its waters, but this is the first time we have actually stepped off the land and followed it; have felt its pull; its relentless crawl to the sea. In some ways it's a strange feeling. I had it as soon as we pushed off, not so much an out-of-body experience as an out-of-land experience. Yet that's not right either, because I've never felt so utterly consumed and engaged with a landscape. I feel like I have been ushered into a world that until now has somehow been hidden. It is as if the river is a vein beneath the skin of the land and has the power to take us into the wild and watery heart of things.

We stop paddling, listening to the trickle-slap, trickle-slap of water on wood. A kingfisher darts overhead in a flash of azure, his shrill *ch-reee* joining the river's quiet song. I hadn't thought about the smells of the river too. This isn't the fierce salt of the sea or the cabbage tang of seaweed, but the delicate, changing scents from wood and water. It is soothing beyond belief.

The trees start to thin out, making way for farmland, and we are joined by a barn owl, following the course of the river banks on her evening hunt. I watch her between strokes. She's delightfully top-heavy, a feathered wedge, like a cartoon body builder. I remember how surprised I was when I first held one, by its lightness, the fragility of its air-filled bones. She has gone by the time we meet a woman standing on a paddle board next to the left bank. We drift past and chat, impressed by her skill and speed on the water, our progress clumsy in comparison. The pub – she tells us – is just five minutes away.

At the Henny Swan we pull the canoe out of the water and upend her by the bank, ordering pints and chips and then eating them by the river. The beer garden is busy, mostly with couples dressed up for a Friday night out in Essex. I feel slightly out of place, puffed up with a life jacket and legs emerald-green with duckweed. James and I talk about the last hour and plot our next trip. We could go overnight. We could follow the river till it scents the sea. We could explore the waterways around where we grew up. We could cross the Channel. The list of possibilities is endless and exciting. A world that just an hour ago felt so utterly explored has cracked wide open.

We make good time back to the Water Meadows, the beer acting as cheery ballast, heaving the canoe onto the bank to watch a teenager spinning for pike. It is a week before the river season begins and he seems nervous about being observed. His cigarette gives off a jazzy fug that suggests pike-poaching isn't his only naughty habit. Within minutes, a patch of water by a lily pad explodes and a great green fish leaps, flumping onto its belly with a crack that sends moorhens hiccupping away in alarm. The rod bends dramatically as the fish torpedoes off, heading for the cover of weeds and then . . . and then nothing. Slack line floats in the warm air like a gossamer thread. The pike has spat the hook.

'Fucking hell! Did you see that?' The boy asks, turning to look at us for the first time, his roll-up hanging from his lip, his face pale and his dark eyes wide under a baseball cap. We smile and nod. Like the pike, our minds are set on returning to the water.

Back home I feel restless and excited. I can't settle to anything. I pull out a stack of maps and look at the vascular bundle of rivers and tributaries spreading out across the county. I know many of the place names which the blue lines skirt round or slice through, but now – and it feels like for the first time – I can also see the miles of landscape, or rather the waterscape, I have missed. I trace them with my fingers and say their names out loud. The Little Ouse, the Waveney, the Stour, the Alde, the Orwell, the Box and the Rat. The Deben, the Dove, the Blyth, the Brett. The Kennett and the Yox. Then there's the Lark, the river that winds its way slowly through where I live now, in Bury St Edmunds. I move my finger down and find the Colne, welling up near Great Yeldham and striking out for my childhood home of Halstead. A river that is as homely as it is mysterious. A flow that has poured into my life, shaping me as surely as the mud of its meandering banks. But its route and the wildlife it contains were things I never really thought of. Although the river runs for 60 miles or more, for me, framed by my blinkered consciousness, it might as well have been just been a matter of yards. I feel now that I was missing the very things which made it special. What's more, the same is true of nearly every river I have experienced. If these blue ribbons were a national park I would have barely pulled into the car park.

A plan begins to form in my mind. I will attempt to explore the country again by canoe – first my country, the places I thought until so recently I knew so well; to rewrite a psychogeography made mean and narrow by the habits of land. But also I want to go further, to paddle along the great rivers that have inspired, moved and licked the land into shape. Places where it is still possible to get lost while knowing exactly where you are. It will be a quiet exploration of the UK, from the smallest tributaries to stent-straight canals and thick arteries that pump towards the sea. Over chalk, gravel, clay and mud. Through fields, woodland, villages, towns and cities to experience places that might otherwise go unnoticed and perhaps unloved. Not only that, but many rivers are also borders. While being on a river is sensually different, lowering us wet-bottomed into an eddying world of green water, it strikes me that it is also a place of freedom. A no man's land between counties and countries, where it is possible to stray briefly outside society, the only law being the pull of paddle against the current. Onwards. Onwards.

I start to scribble down river after river and phone James to tell him; to invite him along. We check calendars and list rivers: the Wye; the Thames; the Lark; somewhere, anywhere in Scotland. With the right planning, we can explore at least ten, maybe more, in a year, fitting in the trips around work and family. Not just in the summer but throughout the winter too: to experience rivers in every season, come rain or shine, hell or high water. I can feel the excitement rising in me at the idea of a vision being brought to life, seeing that the next twelve months will be shaped by the flow of rivers across the country.

We talk about equipment we will need too: stoves, tent, water-proofs, bags, spare paddles. But I know as I'm talking to James that I will also want to do some of these trips alone, to have, I suppose, an experience. Even in solitude I know I shall have company: those that came before, those who ventured onto rivers for nothing more than pure, sparkling pleasure. I will join a precious band who venture forth in lurid waterproofs and boats of garish colours. To ride the waters. To discover the secret network of ways into another world. To feel the pull of the river.

CHAPTER 1

A secret world

The heron has been in front of us all day. It could, of course, be a succession of different herons, but somehow it's comforting to think we've had constant company: a guide. He's standing now near the right bank, both legs planted in the water up to grey-skinned knees – his neck echoing the curves of the river. We put our paddles across our knees and let the water push us towards him. The canoe, in all her shock-red glory, is not a vessel of stealth, but she glides almost silently, the water breaking under her hull with the slightest wet whisper, like sleigh bells tinkling on the river bed. We are close, really close: able to see the sharpness of the heron's dagger bill, his white-and-black-streaked throat and dandyish crest, Brylcreemed flat. He doesn't move. Not a muscle. Just. Waits.

The heron is a symbol of grace, patience, solitude and strength, loved and mistrusted in equal measure. According to

Ovid, he is a pallid bird birthed from Ardea's still-warm ashes, a fish-gulping sinner reborn. Comfortable in water, land and air, an emblem of the otherworld. The poacher of the pond. The king of the river. His is a jumble of stories rooted in our history and attachments to time and place. But one thing I'm sure of, this is his world: hidden and secret. It is a world, though, I hope to sink into and explore, to become as much a part of the river as he is.

We had chosen to start our journeys on the River Waveney. Although not far away from my home, it is a river I don't think I've ever explored; certainly not in any meaningful way. And yet, I do feel I have an emotional connection to it. I was living in Brighton when I first heard *Cigarette on the Waveney*. One of two programmes Roger Deakin made for Radio 4 in 2005, it is an audio diary of a canoe journey down the upper stretch of the Waveney. At a time when my world was one of sea and shingle, salt and brine, the programme, with its descriptions of clear water, of willows and skittering mayfly, was a reminder of the rivers I had grown up with. It made me realise I had somehow lost touch with the rivers in my life – perhaps I had never really understood them at all.

Last week I decided to visit the British Archive for Contemporary Writing at the University of East Anglia, pretty much the only place that holds a copy of *Cigarette on the Waveney*.* I had sat for hours in a glass-fronted room looking through three grey cardboard boxes that contained a sizeable portion of Roger Deakin's life. Letters, postcards, specifications for a custom-made wetsuit, emails and handwritten pages, littered with crossings-out and coffee rings. Some of the notes were made during the time he was working on *Waterlog*, his most famous work. A journey of swims across sea, lakes, rivers, streams, tarns, lochs and lidos, the book became a word-of-mouth classic, not only for its evocative prose but also for its defence of the right to roam. Inspired by John Cheever's short story 'The Swimmer', *Waterlog* was Deakin's personal quest to 'follow the rain on its meanderings' and escape 'endlessly turning back on myself like a tiger pacing its cage'.

There were pictures too. Images of Deakin's home at Walnut Tree Farm in Mellis, Suffolk, where he lived for thirty-eight years, the shepherd huts he used to write in and even the dilapidated cars he drove into hedges – leaving them to be claimed by families of foxes, or hidden by thickets of climbing roses. And, of course there were photos of him swimming, both in the infamously cold moat that surrounded his house and in the River Waveney. Invariably he is doing the breast stroke, his hair a dandelion puff of white sticking out above the dark green of the water. Deakin described this, his favoured

---

* *Cigarette on the Waveney* is available again via the BBC's iPlayer.

swimming style, as the 'naturalist's stroke'. From this position in the water he had a 'frog's eye' view of the unfolding waterscape, allowing him to spy everything: from the tennis-ball-size holes of water voles in the bank to the fat chub scudding along the river bottom.

The boxes contained other things. Unexpected and delightful things. I took out a square of neatly folded stretchy fabric nestled deep within layers of tissue paper, like some hibernating creature. The colour of the sea at night, a deep, depthless blue, I felt as if I was holding Deakin's second skin: the Turin Shroud of wild swimming, his favourite pair of Speedos. For a reason I still cannot quite explain, perhaps hoping for the faint scent of river, I even took a quick sniff.

I found the recording I came for in the third and final box. I slipped the CD into my laptop and pulled on the headphones, smiling as I heard the trickle of water, then Deakin's voice bubbling softly like river over stone. It was just as I remembered it: 'The Waveney for me as my local river has always been an escape route. A way into another world.'

I listened again and again, soaking up his words, as well as the moments where he lets the river talk. Some of the most evocative parts of the recording are simply the sound of water under the canoe, the chuckling drip of dipped paddles as Deakin eased himself into a hidden, more contemplative world.

Like *Waterlog*, *Cigarette on the Waveney* also has a literary undercurrent, in that it was partly inspired by a voyage made by Robert Louis Stevenson and his friend Sir Walter Grindlay Simpson. In 1876 the pair had set off to explore the rivers and canals of Belgium and northern France, Stevenson paddling the oak Arethusa and Simpson manning a sleek cedar-wood canoe called the Cigarette – the name Deakin chose for his own much-loved Canadian canoe. He said this homage meant he always had an 'imaginary companion, paddling alongside in a ghostly sort of way'. For me this is another reason to retrace Deakin's route. There is a hope that by following his paddle strokes, I will have a similar kind of spiritual connection – if not to the man, then at least to the waterscape he loved.

We start paddling again, following the heron as he rises from the water, a half-run, half-leap into the air and a flap of oil-black primary feathers outstretched like fingers hammered flat. We're beginning to find our stride as we delve deeper into river country.

Actually getting on the river this morning had proved much harder than we had anticipated. We had wanted to be as close to the source as possible so headed for a road bridge a few miles from Redgrave. I had expected it to be scenic and rural, the river bucolic and bubbling, but just off the main road we were surrounded by houses. The hedges along the river bank were thick and unwelcoming, their inch-long thorns decorated with litter and a grim bunting made from discarded bags of dog poo. A towering phalanx of nettles scuppered any last hope of easy access. Even where we could see the water, it didn't seem to hold much promise for exploring. The weather, hot and dry all week, had left the river desperately low, with hardly enough water to wet the canoe's bottom, let alone float it. The canoe, now named the Pipe in a wry nod to Deakin, Stevenson and Simpson, would have to stay strapped to the roof of my Fiesta like some absurd red Mohican.

In the end we were rescued by the generosity of a camp-site owner, who allowed us to launch on his land. He stood by good-humouredly as we packed the canoe with a rag-tag mix of back-packs in bin-liners and Waitrose carrier bags before sliding her into the water. It felt momentous. The start of something. But also, it was a reminder of how new we are to this. We sweated as we tried to rediscover the rhythm we thought we had mastered on the Stour, ducking branches and making splashed, awkward strokes. Passing through Oakley and Scole, we lay flat on our backs under low-slung crack willows that knocked off our hats and dragged at our clothes, laughing as we sat back up festooned in catkins like fat, fluffy caterpillars. The water rushed over mud and gravel rapids before becoming slowly deeper – moving from lively source to beautiful rural river.

Now we find ourselves on a stretch where the tall banks can be touched with an outstretched paddle from either side, meaning the slightest wrong move leads to a close and painful brush with nettles and reed. But it also gives us the first real sense of being on, or even in the river, of unfamiliar surroundings to explore and discover. The overhanging vegetation creates the impression that we are sliding down a long green tube: tunnel-vision into a watery world.

For this whole trip we will be in border country. To the left, Norfolk, and to the right, as far as Herringfleet, Suffolk. To be skirting both, to be effectively no place at all, feels powerful and exciting. It is to be somehow outside of society. It reminds me of when Huckleberry Finn and Jim slip onto the Mississippi in their home-made craft: 'So in two seconds away we went a-sliding down the river, and it did seem so good to be free again and all by ourselves on the big river, and nobody to bother us.'

Downstream, even before the tidal pull kicks in, the Waveney is a true Broadland river, busy with pleasure craft that cut creamy lines through the water. But here it is quiet enough to hear fish plopping to the surface and the whisper of reeds. The swans certainly seem surprised by the company, taking it in turns to race us in relay. For five minutes at a time they stay 30 feet ahead of us, before shuffling onto the bank and allowing another to take up the slow pursuit, white tails raised and wagging at us in a regal taunt. But the feathered pacemakers give us our rhythm and soon it feels that it is the paddle, not the arm that's leading, the wood enjoying the taste of the water. As he made his way down Belgium's canals Stevenson described canoeing as easy work. It's a passage Deakin quoted as he paddled down the Waveney: 'Dipping at the proper inclination, now right, now left, to empty a little pool in the nap of the apron. There's not much art in that. Certain silly muscles managed it between sleep and waking and meanwhile the brain had a whole holiday and went to sleep.'

The river begins to widen here and we can glimpse water meadow as the steep banks fall back. The solidity of grass and mud is replaced by the softness of reed, the tight, tortuous bends finally easing.

Not far from Billingsford, we limbo under a bridge, the rush of stony-cold air delicious in the heat. An otter has been here too, a faint trail can be seen in the mud along with an old spraint: a crumbly, fishy cigar of pearly scale and hair-thin bone. We stop nearby for lunch, heaving the Pipe through mud that swallows our legs to the shin, guffing out a sulphurous pong when we pull them free. We eat sandwiches with our legs dangling in the water, partly to wash away the stink, but also still to feel the river's gentle pull, desperate not to leave completely this new, sparkling world.

Pushing on, we repeat Deakin's incantation of place names from *Cigarette on the Waveney*: Wortham, Roydon, Diss, Scole, Billingford, Hoxne, Brockdish. The rhythm of the words matches the strokes of the paddle, and our muscles return to working almost without thought, our brains only woken from slumber with the hiccup of a moorhen or the hissed warning of a swan, its back laden with fluffy grey cygnets.

The river is truly alive, its inhabitants scurrying about their business, ignoring the interlopers intruding on their world. From watercress, reeds and hemlock rise dizzying clouds of banded demoiselles. One amorous pair take a break from acrobatic mid-air copulation and land on the front of the canoe, their blue bodies still locked together and their fluttering wings marked with a black spot like an inky fingerprint. James stops paddling to reach for another stranded in the water, placing it gently on a clump of reeds to dry out.

'A damsel in distress,' he says, grinning.

The water is full of lilies too. Their buttery, bright-yellow flowers are tightly closed, but their buds periscope out of the water like stalked alien eyes charting our progress. The paddles disturb their submerged leaves, causing them to swirl, as Deakin had described, like 'crumpled underwear' in a washing machine. We pass the mile to Hoxne almost in silence, brains soothed by the soft trickle of water passing underneath the Pipe's heavy bow. It is a beautiful stretch of river, willow and alders bending over the water while kingfishers shoot overhead like wobbling gas flames: afterburners on full. The heron again. We glide along, our senses saturated and soaked as we explore and discover all that the world of the river has to offer.

The old mill at Hoxne is imposing but beautiful, moving from brick to white wooden weatherboarding by the second of its three storeys. The chimney from the neighbouring steam shed matches the mill for height; it seems like a strange industrial interloper in this rural spot. We leave the official Environment Agency-sanctioned portage point a small distance behind us, intent on manhandling the Pipe over the weir and following after, rather than tramping for some distance with bare legs through dense stands of nettles. But closer to the weir the flow is surprisingly strong, and we fear that dropping from its steep step onto the concrete apron below might do lasting damage to both the canoe and us. We stop by a bank and get out onto carefully mown grass.

'We're in someone's garden,' hisses James as we grab hold of the front of the canoe and drag it at top speed across the grass, the paddles bumping and clanking. The house is some distance away and doesn't look lived in, but the grounds have clearly been tended – even if the glass greenhouse we huff and puff past is almost exploding with weeds, their green heads pushing sadly against cracked panes. With a last guilty look over our shoulders, we belly-slide the Pipe back into the water, scrambling down the bank behind her, drenching our legs and most of our gear in our haste to get away.

It was close to here where Deakin made his camp when he canoed the Waveney. He paddled the Cigarette up the mill race to a spot that in late summer is full of giant puffballs. He described seeing so many they looked 'like the rows of bare bottoms of swimmers getting changed'. I had thought we'd stay at the same location. But it's nowhere near the halfway point, and if we are to reach Geldeston tomorrow we need to keep going.

Downstream, near Syleham, we come to a part of the river where someone has taken great care to string 'Private, no entry' signs across the banks. Even the weir is decorated with a prohibitive notice. We stop paddling, wondering if we have taken a wrong turn somewhere. We haven't. We can't have. Turning round, we head back to what we thought was the mill race in the hope that there is some way through. Close to the bank there are a number of houses, no doubt associated with the mill.

We ease past the moored boats but the route is a dead end. We try and turn round again, now mightily pissed off, but the length of the Pipe is almost exactly the same as the width of the channel. Her nose jams on the mud of the north bank while her stern rams noisily into the moored boats. Mud. Clonk. Mud. Clonk.

A voice comes from the bank.

'Can I help?'

The sour expression on the woman's face and the cutting tone say something completely different.

'You are not on the Waveney now, you know . . .' she continues, not waiting for our reply. We stop trying to extricate ourselves from our tight spot and twist round to face her, trying to look as innocent as possible.

'Where are we then?'

She puts her hands on her hips authoritatively.

'Well, technically this water belongs to the mill and all of the houses along here. If you want to get on the river you have to get the canoe out at one of the moorings back there, which are also private, and then take it across the car park.' She sucks her lip, thinking. 'You can then get back onto the river on the other side.'

I look at James. The 'private' mooring she is talking about is some distance away and, factoring in the car park, the suggested route over land would mean heaving the Pipe about 500 yards – a good 495 yards further than I'm willing to travel.

'Where are you going anyway?' says the woman.

James patiently explains what we are doing. How we hope to reach Geldeston, how the trip is about retracing one of Roger Deakin's trips and exploring river country. The woman's face brightens and she smiles broadly for the first time.

'Oh you'll never make it,' she says cheerfully. 'The most I've managed is three miles and that took for ever. Oh dear me yes, you won't be able to get through.'

We thank her through gritted teeth and paddle away.

'Only for the brave,' she warbles after us, 'only for the brave.'

We go back to the weir with the sign. There's something about these notices that is deeply annoying; antagonistic even, especially on a river that is so quiet. We haven't seen a soul on the water since we left – or on the Angles Way footpath that follows its course – so it's hardly as if someone's peace will be shattered by an illicit portage. On the Waveney there is an agreement in place between landowners and fishing clubs to allow navigation by canoe and kayak with a British Canoeing licence, something we both have. I can't help but worry. If we're encountering problems here, I wonder how easy it is going to be on the other rivers. Could it be that the secret windows I hope to find, the waterscapes I hope to experience, are locked down and guarded? So much for messing about on the river.

James and I hold the canoe steady and discuss what to do. The sign has already cost us a good half-hour of forward progress. The only option is to go over the weir. The water is shallow as we get out and heave the Pipe onto the concrete step, clambering up after her to stand dripping on the weed-splattered slope. We crouch behind and push, following the canoe down at uncontrolled speed, the smooth soles of our wetsuit boots skating over the algal slime, landing us shouting in the water. 'Only for the brave!' we trill. Although I laugh, the words have put me on edge. We are on a tight schedule for this trip and our canoe is undoubtedly more substantial than the craft the woman used. We push on in silence, past Needham Mill and another weir that announces its unwelcome presence with a waterfall song.

The river seems more open now, the trees retreating. We scud by at eye-level with the banks, udder height with the cows that now stamp about in every field. My arms are tiring; it feels like they have been stretched, my body wearily resigned to concertina-ing its way forward. My backside is killing me too, the fat of each cheek has been tenderised to the bone. I don't want to let James down so I keep quiet, but I can see he is tiring too and it's not long before we start to look for somewhere to camp. Twice we stop, springing from the canoe to inspect a possible location, only to think again after spotting cows in the distance. I know that as soon as they see us they will be in to investigate, trampling our gear (and probably us) with clumsy, bovine benevolence.

It is the barn owl who leads us to the perfect spot. Flying along the bank, she turns and flies inland. We decide to follow her, leaping from the canoe onto a tree whose exposed roots make a perfect step. Using our last ounce of strength we drag the Pipe up the bank behind us, the cow-churned mud farting noisily beneath our feet. The field is cut in two by a dyke and there is a road about 300 yards away, more of a track really, leading past the field and to some houses nearby. Part of me worries about a farmer seeing us and asking us to leave; the other part is simply too tired to care.

James puts up the tent while I sort out the stove, lighting the meth burner with a satisfying pop. I feel the heat with the palm of my hand before putting a pan of water on top.

We eat pasta and drink generous slugs of rum from tin mugs, the alcohol sending a ribbon of warmth into my chest as the last of the light slips away. The land is dark, the river darker. The barn owl returns to check on us just as we are turning in, ghosting over an old willow with a silent flutter of wings that flash powder-white through to graphite and caramel, her face a perfect feathered heart.

In the tent we lie in our sleeping bags like landlocked caddis flies, marooned but cosy, chatting in low voices and listening to the sounds of the night. As Deakin did on his canoe trip, we hear the distant bark of a fox, but there is something else too. A chittering, huffing noise. Somewhere between asleep and waking I imagine it is an otter that has clawed up the bank to investigate our camp, rolling in the long grass and playing in the shelter beneath our canoe. The sound comes again. Hum-hum-hum. Hum-hum-hum-hum. The noise fades away behind the whispering rustle of wind-ruffled canvas. I think of the otter humping away across the field to belly-slide down the muddy bank into the water. A gift from the Waveney.

The morning brings mist and a herd of suspicious cows, staring at us with dark eyes while we hurriedly pack. I have no idea what the time is, but I can't help but wonder if the farmer sent the girls in to remove the campers from his land. James tips the canoe into the water while I stand protecting our gear, holding a paddle like a staff and meekly telling the cows to 'Please, get out of it.' They don't seem bothered. The bovine circle is getting tighter and tighter, and one with large swivelling eyes snuffles into one of our food bags, wiping thick strands of egg-white drool over my backpack. They are still coming forward, heads swinging, their numbers bolstered by latecomers eager to push to the front to see what all the fuss is about. I throw the last of the bags to James and scramble down the bank as the cows finally break ranks to form a beefy wall at the water's edge. They low a soft 'good riddance' as we paddle to the centre of the river and skip alongside us before turning their attention back to the serious business of chewing the cud. I think again of *Cigarette on the Waveney*, of Deakin's experience with the cows on the bank, his laughter at their sugar-plum fairy routines, his bellows of 'Hello girls.'

It is a relief to sink back into our watery world. The light is softer here, the sounds muffled. Even in our remote camping spot we could still hear the occasional car and the low rumble of a milk tanker. But now, screened by the banks, the noise of roads is replaced with ripples and the lulling shush of water on wood. This is the escape route that Deakin was speaking of, the secret window I was so hoping to find. A different plane of existence that runs through the towns and landmarks of a county that, until now, I thought I knew so well. I notice James has stopped paddling as he scans the meandering river ahead. I put my hand on his shoulder and we let the Pipe glide slowly along, fully immersed in the riverscape. Cows seem to greet us on every shoulder of land, jostling for space to stare at us, or in the case of one particularly grumpy-looking bull, bellowing with enough force to send a moorhen sprinting across the water in alarm.

Mendham Mill is about half an hour from where we camped, a vast wooden ship beached on a low horizon of river and water meadow. We get out at the portage point by the mill's weir and inspect a sign erected for canoeists by the Environment Agency. The instructions, formal to the point of shirtiness, instruct paddlers to walk through a field of cows to the left. I go ahead to check it out, following the path through the field, across a road, eventually reaching a wooden platform by the river. It is at least 500 yards of uneven terrain. I walk back looking at the river, waving cheerily to someone standing at the open doorway of the mill house, his pink chinos clashing with ruddy cheeks. He ignores me, but follows my route along the bank with his eyes, lips pursed and disapproving. I can't help but get the feeling that those living by the river view those who use it with deep suspicion; as if it is a personal moat to their castles. This hidden world is not one they want to share.

Directly under the weir, the Waveney riffles over shallows before shooting through the millpond and under a bridge. There's a good place to put the canoe in too, even if it will mean going shin-deep in mud. I check the EA sign again, its authoritative tone only lightened by an illustration of a canoeist happily hoicking his craft above his head. I think of the spine-crunching repercussions if we attempted such an athletic manoeuvre with the Pipe. It is James who makes the decision for both of us: 'Sod that, let's just go the shortest route.'

The sun has burnt off the last of the mist as we get back into the canoe, the mud from our feet congealing with the cow-slobber on our bags. Last night, as the light began to fall, the river had felt lonely at times, even melancholy, but now we've entered a different world again, another riverscape to explore; it has become a place of tremendous fun. The deep-green depths have been replaced by clear shallows that rocket and sing; chattering and turning pebbles to disturb bullheads and caddis-fly nymphs. Several times we jump out to skip the Pipe over tiny stone weirs, mindful that our walking speed is probably faster than our paddling. Damselflies, stirred into life by the sun, rise in clouds, some skimming the water in front of the canoe like little sprites leading us on. I feel stupidly happy. There is nowhere I'd rather be than outdoors and wandering with the Pipe. Stevenson obviously felt the same on his trip, asking rhetorically, 'For will anyone dare to tell me that business is more entertaining than fooling among boats?'

But for Stevenson, like us, there were also those who said his little exploration could not be done. Shortly before Landrecies a 'vivacious old man' told him he would not be able to pass all the locks along the canal, advising him to 'Get into a train, my little man . . . and go you away home to your parents.' Stevenson, who said he was 'inwardly fuming', insisted he would now complete the trip 'in spite of him . . . just because he had dared to say we could not'. Thinking back to the Syleham woman's warning from last night, my concerns disappear. If these joyful shallows were the barrier to her progress, then we are home and dry.

The river slowly, reluctantly, deepens and we watch a pike hanging almost motionless by the Norfolk bank, a dirty green torpedo packed with a mouthful of needles. But as the depth returns the width disappears. The river becomes narrow enough for fallen crack willows to span the banks, and countless times we lie on our backs to squeeze through a narrow space, the branches scratching at our faces and depositing rafts of spiders into the canoe. Thick banks of reeds furred with biting gnats cut the channel in two. Whichever route we take means clomping through reeds and sending big black balloons of teeth up into the air that come down to engulf our heads and arms. Their song, their buzz, enters my bones. Even the water feels thick with it. The barrage is relentless.

I always intended to swim along the journey, but my first dip is unexpected. Passing under a low-slung willow I lose my balance and topple head-first into the water. The water roars into my ears, great green bubbles popping in front of my eyes. Surprise and panic give way to delight as I bob to the surface like a cork. I tell myself off for being momentarily scared, my love of the water overtaken by a sense that the canoe is a place of a safety that must not be left at any point. The water is refreshing but not cold and feels silky next to my skin. It is too deep to touch the bottom, so I swim slowly to the bank where

James, grinning, manoeuvres the canoe alongside and I clamber clumsily back in. I feel like the mythical fox who lowered himself into a river to drown his fleas. But back on board the gnats come for me again, a toothy rebuke for my watery escape.

We stop just past Homersfield, spread out our map and clumsily try to measure the route with spaced fingers. We're still discussing how many hours it will take to reach Bungay when we spot the canoe coming towards us, the first people we have seen on the river since we set out. A couple in their late fifties, the woman in front is hammering along, her paddles sending up great geysers of green water, while her husband grimly tries to keep pace. We wave gamely from the bank and the man, with a look of relief, takes it as a cue to stop paddling. He explains that they too are heading upstream to Bungay and plan to get the bus back to their starting point of Homersfield, a route they've completed numerous times. It is an odd conversation, him shouting over his shoulder, his wife – still paddling furiously – dragging them downstream.

'You're taking the canoe on the bus?' James shouts after them.

'Oh yes, no problem at all.' He pauses and twists right round to look at us. Studying us hard.

'You know, you're the first people we've ever seen canoeing from here. Lots of people after Bungay, but never here.'

He starts to say something else, but decides against it, instead waving again and turning back to face the river and the back of his wife's head. They're soon out of sight; the river is once again ours alone to explore.

I still can't get over how the river changes; from trickle to muscular pulse, from lively and low to broad-backed and still. It feels living and adaptable, not something that is just part of the landscape but something that forms it, moves it, makes it. It is from the river that the land makes sense. To journey along it is, in some curious way, to sense old time. We paddle slowly, the flow now broad and dark, bordered by great corridors of trees along the bank. The branches glow green with the sun behind them. It is the light of fairy tales, of magic. A different world again.

I feel at home here in a way that I never have before on water. When I lived in Brighton I made a couple of stabs at kayaking off the coast, but I never could get my sea legs. The short time I did manage to stay inside the kayak I felt ground down by the sheer monotony of the sea, with its endless humps of grey water that slapped moodily against the plastic hull. The lumpy Channel left me feeling pathetically ill, twice forcing me to return to the shingle beach to be violently sick in a bin.

We stop for lunch in sight of Bungay. The setting is beautiful (a word that, in correspondence with *Cigarette on the Waveney*'s producer, Deakin apologised for overusing). The river snakes through lush meadows. It feels like nothing has changed here for centuries. Over the trees to the right I can see a church. I wonder if it is St Mary's, where Shuck, the Black Dog of Bungay, a creature with burning red eyes and fur so oily it cast a reflection, was said to have appeared in the summer of 1577. Legend has it that on the day of Shuck's most notorious appearance, a violent thunderstorm darkened the skies and shook the church with such 'rain, hail, thunder and lightning as was never seen the like'. The people inside the church were said to have been kneeling in fear when ol' Shuck appeared before them. Surrounded by an aura of fire, the beast rampaged through the church snapping at the congregation with dagger-like teeth, bringing death on swift heels. The Reverend Abraham Fleming, whose tale *A Straunge and Terrible Wunder* claims to be based on contemporary oral accounts, said the 'black dog, or the divel' ran with 'great swiftnesse, and incredible haste, among the people'. The beast passed between two kneeling in prayer and 'wrung the necks of them bothe', while a third 'shrivelled up like a drawn purse' after being grazed by the beast's hellish flanks. Shuck left the church to reappear seven miles away in Blythburgh, 'slaying two men and a lad' and leaving his sooty scratch marks in the church's wooden door.

Academics, who have no conscience when it comes to ruining a good story, have suggested that the fierce electrical storm, coupled with the trauma of the ongoing Reformation, may have given birth to the legend. The beast a living metaphor for uncertainty: fear made flesh. But Shuck still lives on in Bungay. The black dog leaps across the top of the town's crest and snarls from weather vanes. His unearthly speed is remembered in the name of the running club. Sightings of Shuck occasionally still occur, not just here, but across East Anglia when the storm clouds race in over the flatlands and lightning burns across the sky.

It is easy paddling through the deep meanders that lead us under crumbling red-brick bridges to the looming flint walls of the derelict Bungay Castle. The river, shallow again and thick with fish that leap and shoot past us, gushes over gravel and stone. After almost two solid days of rural canoeing, gliding past gardens is somewhat strange. It is another secret world, one of patios and sheds, washing lines and back windows.

The river grows steadily deeper and broader as it loops around the town like a watery lasso. Without any wind the water looks like a sheet of dark volcanic glass, reflecting trees, birds and hedges. The river is swelling to fill every sense and it's hard to tell real from reflection. The horizon is dizzying, fluid and coppery. The spell is only broken by the arrival of the rain. A bone-shaking thunderclap followed by marble-sized drops of water that cause the river to dance and boil. James and I shiver into waterproof jackets and paddle into the storm, gliding under trees when we can for a respite from the aerial barrage.

There is plenty of evidence of how the water levels change with the weather. Previous deluges have stacked sticks and silt against the low-lying branches, creating muddy beaver dams that we are forced to clamber over, swearing, heaving the heavy hulk of the Pipe behind us. We go from riparian to arboreal in the blink of an eye.

The rain is showing no signs of easing. Muddy puddles an inch deep are forming in the bottom of the Pipe. I grab an old water bottle and cut into it with a knife, forming two makeshift bailers. I pass one to James and we take it in turns to paddle while the other slops the brown water over the side. We barely talk, a palpable grump descending on us with the clouds. The rain makes the river world seem smaller, tighter: all is water. It rained during Deakin's trip too, not a downpour but a shower, creating a 'raindrop ballet all the way down the river'.

By Outney Common, the river splits in front of us and it's hard to tell where to go. Both channels seem of similar size and we pull into the bank to look at the map. The wind and rain whip it to rags as soon as I open it, so I clamber out to try and find shelter behind the roots of a fallen tree. The map is next to useless. Every attempt to read it causes it to tear and gum together, the roads and rivers of Bungay fusing with those of Lowestoft. I stuff it into a bag and head back to the canoe. We pick a direction and set off, trying not to think of how it would feel to have to retrace our steps. The rain is so hard now it hurts my head, forcing me to stop paddling to wipe the water from my eyes. It feels like we are in the way of the natural cycle, an obstacle to be overcome. I count the seconds between thunder and the forks of lightning that cut a ragged path from grey cloud to sodden earth. It's good weather for Shucks.

Past the Bungay loop, a sense of quiet returns to the river. It is as if the rain has transformed the landscape, washing everything away to leave a dull expanse of almost featureless farmland. The water is the only active thing, but it still offers plenty to be discovered, the surface blistered from rising fish and coloured with the dashing blue of yet more damselflies, humming and flittering on rustling paper wings.

As the afternoon begins to fade towards evening the low hum of biting insects slowly cranks up. Mosquitoes, with their undercarriage of skinny legs already lowered, launch repeated bloody sorties on the backs of our necks and arms. The rhythm of our paddles is joined with syncopated slaps and curses. Our saviours arrive soon after. Swallows, clicking and twittering, shoot overhead, their glossy blue-black backs catching the light as they dive towards the water, pulling up at the last moment – tails streaming out behind them like jet trails. I feel like a Blitzed Londoner watching the arrival of Spitfires.

We tackle weirs with greater enthusiasm now, more confident at what the boat can accomplish, but also knowing each one is a concrete step towards the end point. Ellingham weir, the start of the tidal reach, is the last on the route and we actually celebrate the sight of its battered grey face looming out of the water. We glide over to the right bank and get out, dog-tired from ten hours of canoeing and still uncomfortably damp from the deluge. I pad over to an Environment Agency sign by the road bridge to see how many miles we have to walk with the Pipe. It's worse than I thought. There is no access to the river at all. The drop from the weir is big, possibly 12 feet to where gigantic slabs of river come crashing down to continue its race to the sea. We abandon the Pipe and decide to set out along the road to see if there is a way we can walk the canoe to a launching point. After five minutes we stop. There is no way we can carry the boat that far.

James is dejected.

'Looks like this is it,' he says, taking off his life vest. It's hard to see what else we can do. It was here that Deakin described walking through 'armies of nettles' that left his legs on fire, but there was no mention of this gigantic concrete hurdle. By the road I notice a small gate, padlocked closed with a 'No admittance' sign, which leads to a small grassy path that hugs the road bridge before bending down towards the river. I jump over to explore and soon find a small ledge above the water. It is still a good distance above the river – perhaps about five feet – but the buttresses of the weir are covered in corrugated pieces of metal that reach from the path to the waterline.

If we can just get the Pipe over the gates and nose-dive her into the water, it's possible we can use this part of the weir as a ladder.

I walk back to James, who has gone back to staring into the water. I explain the route and he seems to recover instantly, emptying the canoe and almost dragging it to the gates single-handed. It takes about half an hour to get her up and over and back into the water. A group of men with slicked-back hair sit in a dark estate car and watch, smoking cigarettes and occasionally laughing behind their hands.

We are exhausted by the time we get underway again, gliding under two weeping willows that form a green curtain to the tidal stretch. We dig deep, looking for the sweet spot, the Pipe zipping over the flat water. Her nose never wavers now, she is leading us home. The sky is darkening to an ominous plum that suggests we are in for another downpour, the last light of the day sucked into spongy clouds. The first fat spots are landing when we arrive at the Geldeston Locks Inn. Wet and exhausted, we order a pint and squelch back outside the pub where the Pipe is pulled up on the riverside.

We sit in comfortable, companionable silence, listening to folk music coming from the sagging marquee in the beer garden, the river mumbling on. This is where and how Deakin finished his trip, toasting the Cigarette, Robert Louis Stevenson and the Arethusa with a pint. We echo his words and raise our glasses with paddle-sore arms one final time.

'Here's to Roger, here's to the Pipe and here's to the next voyage.'

I thought we would both be elated, but it is strange stepping back into this world. Floating beings, our brains have been transported in a bubble of water that popped as soon as we reached land; letting in the noise and rush of people and cars. It feels like it's not just land we have been outside of, but time too. The river is a place where the drip of time both speeds up and slows down, where minutes and hours melt away into the water. I definitely feel closer to the river than when we set out. The river has opened up to me. Or perhaps it is I that have opened to the river. I've let its water rush through my skin and bones, filling me up. The unexpected dunking, an embrace or a baptism. The heron the long-necked priest.

Deakin was right: a river can be a secret window, and I want to hold it open for as long as I can.

CHAPTER 2

Escape routes

Part of the pull of the river is escape. To paddle on a river is to break into a new world, one that feels free from the usual rules and confines of human society. On the water you are not a journalist, a father, an artist or a friend. The salesman is drowned, the doctor turned to bubbling, wind-whipped foam, the office walls overcome and overwhelmed in a surging flood. We are free to wander, alone and unchecked. Although there are only ever two ways to go, the possibilities seem endless. We are outside civilisation, away from it all.

Today we're heading downstream, towards Dedham, Flatford and the sea. The Stour was a river we had to return to. Two visits to the river with two names: the Stower (*stoo-er*) if you're standing on the Suffolk bank, or the Stour (*st-hour*) if you're washed up on the Essex side. Not only is it a river that both of us have grown up alongside, it is also the route of one of the country's biggest mass paddles, a watery version of the

Kinder Scout trespass. Started during the 1970s by the Stour River Trust, a charity formed to safeguard river access, it was originally called 'The Length of the River Cruise'. Now known as 'Sudbury to the Sea', the route follows 24½ miles from Sudbury to the Cattawade Barrier, which cleaves the wriggling worm of the river in two: the fresh-water body from the salty head.

The event is, in some ways, simply a chance to get on the river to see large swathes of countryside inaccessible by foot or road. It is an adventure. But it is also a pointed demonstration of use that helps protect the Stour's navigability, enshrined in statute since 1705 and probably threatened ever since. We had thought about taking part this year, to join the annual migration downstream and talk to people about their connection with the river, their reasons for signing up. But the idea of being part of a paddling peloton doesn't sit well. For this time at least, we want to make our own way, our own discoveries, to register our own very polite and very legal protest.

I must admit, before I started paddling, I hadn't realised the question of access was such a contentious one. As far as I was aware, the banks and the beds may be owned but the water is nobody's – or rather, it is everyone's. Yet some would argue that the water is owned just as much as the land: the rivers are moats, exclusive businesses or personal playgrounds.

While in Scotland (and many other European countries) there is a public right to access non-tidal rivers, across England and Wales there is undisputed access to just 4 per cent of rivers.

That's roughly 1,400 miles of largely slow-moving water out of the 42,700 available. Hardly an example of freedom. But to journey elsewhere, according to landlords, particularly anglers and angling clubs, is to commit trespass – a civil offence that allows landowners to seek damages or an injunction. A glance at internet forums suggests that a quicker, nastier justice can also be meted out, with leaded lines and barbed hooks. In fact both the Angling Trust and River Access For All, a website formed by three canoeists to generate awareness about navigation rights, have conflict maps and dossiers of evidence charting watery disputes. The river, it seems, is a battleground.

Over the past fifteen years things have come to a head. The Rev. Dr Douglas Caffyn, whose MA and PhD focused on historic river access, made waves when he claimed that non-tidal rivers (there is no dispute over access to tidal parts of rivers) have always been public and nothing in law has ever been done to change that. His legal and historic research was enough to convince British Canoeing, and Caffyn quickly became a hero for canoeists and kayakers: a riparian Robin Hood, a freedom fighter who had almost single-handedly given back swathes of the waterscape to the great unwashed. But others, the anglers and no doubt many landowners, saw him as an under-qualified rogue, representative of a militant minority hell-bent on ruining fishing and legitimising trespass.

Caffyn's claims caused such a froth of controversy that the Angling Trust, and then Caffyn himself, hired QCs to support their side of the argument, and the war of words commenced. Papers full of terse arguments swirled back and forth over the meaning of the Magna Carta's order to remove weirs; the relevance of Roman law to English; the similarity of paths to rivers. Both sides claimed victory, or at least refused to admit defeat.

In my mind the exclusion of the public from hundreds of miles of river over vast tracts of the country seems utterly, obviously wrong. River access should not be about money or territorial rights but equality and freedom, to allow people to experience, enjoy and ultimately protect a crucial part of their environment. Importantly, this doesn't mean access to all rivers all the time. Alongside issues of trespass when physically getting onto the river, environmental considerations must also be taken into account (as Caffyn and British Canoeing both recognise), and it is quite possible that some rivers shouldn't be paddled at all.

The issues surrounding the rights of navigation in England and Wales remain fraught and the dispute rumbles on. Perhaps it is time for the government – which expects paddlers and anglers to organise access agreements between themselves on a local basis – to step in. Scotland has already established rights to roam most of its land and inland waters in a move that recognises the need for everyone to be free to explore and enjoy what is a significant and beautiful part of our natural world. After all, rivers are not just of local value; they are of national importance.

Who knows if and when this will ever happen. But until it does, I will paddle as I believe we always have in this country: happily and freely.

Today is our second day on the Stour. Yesterday we paddled through Lamarsh and Bures and camped in a narrow stretch of trees between the water and the fence of a farmer's field, watching the river creep past us like a sheet of glacial ice the colour of hammered tin. This morning we pushed on through a cathedral of trees close to Wissington; the water was so still that we were the centre of a six-dimensional world, unable to tell if the branches that speared from the water were real or reflected. A tree trompe l'oeil, broken only by the darting flight of a kingfisher that flitted from perch to perch, patiently waiting for us to catch up. We passed through gravel shallows that forced us to get out and push, returning to paddle minutes later with ankles and shins livid red with cold, and pushed on again, past Nayland, with its back gardens pressed up to the river and lawns decorated with an armada of landlocked boats.

Now, as we continue our journey and come across the next portage route, we start to see the evidence that we're not entirely welcome. The route winds through a private garden and the signs make it quite clear that access is only given grudgingly. 'No straying from the path.' 'No loitering.' 'No picnics.'

'No urination.' It's a long walk with the Pipe and I can feel my back creaking. We get her in position and James takes over while I stretch out, giving her a hefty push off the launching platform. Her nose dips and bounces as she rushes into the water, belly-flopping with a satisfying crack into the ribbons of ice-smooth water where the current is strongest. She turns one way then another, before bobbing off happily. I look at James.

'Haven't you got the rope?'

His eyes widen in alarm.

'I thought you'd got it.'

We stand watching for a second – watching the current grip the canoe and carry her onwards with more speed than we've managed to muster in a day and a half of solid paddling. She is a riderless horse, kicking up her heels at the lightening of the load. Then James is off after her, flapping hell for leather down the river bank before emerging with a crash of branches further downstream. He bum-slides down the bank, grasping onto trees and shrubs as his feet skate on damp grass and mud, before throwing himself headlong at the Pipe. He lands half in, half out, the Pipe bucking and rolling with displeasure. He is spreadeagled in the canoe, with his body resting on the rear seat, his arms gripping the gunwales and his feet kicking up water as he attempts to pull himself in.

The Pipe turns in slow, shuddering circles in the centre of the river, James starfished across its back end. Then I realise what I'm holding.

'James, I've got both the paddles.'

Silence.

'James?'

A low, wounded-animal moan comes from the canoe, a swear word muffled by the bags in which James's head is now half-buried. The current eventually rescues us, delivering the Pipe and James to a soft bed of reeds.

We head on towards Langham, a place Sir Alfred Munnings described with affection in his autobiography: 'To use the word Arcadia here is not affectation. No other word could describe Langham Mill, its lock, bridge, mill-pool, floodgates and trees . . .'

From 1919 to 1935 Munnings painted here, bathed here, walked along the banks and took to its waters in a rowing boat. But I doubt he would recognise it now. The mill, the lock and the trees are gone; instead the river is funnelled by a steep, gripless concrete V. We have, as usual, ignored the warning sign for the weir, hoping that we might be able to portage the canoe across a shorter distance. But this time it is there for a reason. The water grabs hold of the canoe, shaking her. It feels as if every drop of the river is surging forward in a rush towards the sea. We have little choice but to go with it, pretending to ourselves that we are in control.

The flow is separated by a grey hump like a whale's back breached in the shallows of the Stour, forcing water to foam round its impassable bulk. The current tugs us to the channel on the right and the roar of the water fills my ears, spumes of brown-hued foam flicking over the canoe's sides to land on our legs and chest. I hold my breath and brace my legs against the sides, bringing my body forward as I work the paddle, transfixed and terrified by the yellow-fringed fury of the water. Freeing ourselves from the regular routes is not without its risks.

Then we are over the edge – popped like a cork from a bottle. The fizz of the current bubbles against the Pipe's sides. We are jubilant, reaching forward and back towards each other to try and high-five, the Pipe bouncing around proudly and still travelling at a fair speed. We're both shouting, bodies alive with adrenaline. But the river shouts back. We hadn't seen the second step. We go again, paddling hard to hit the gap that is funnelling a spout of water down to the river below. The Pipe wobbles and bucks before taking the plunge, her nose sinking almost to the bottom before springing joyously to the surface. But the washing-machine current isn't done with us yet, and forces the back end of the canoe round until we are sent spinning down the river, slowly rotating through 360 degrees like a giant wooden clock hand turning in the autumn sun.

Drunk with exhilaration and eager to talk about the experience over tea and food, we decide to stop. I set up the stove and we sit with our backs to trees frilled with beefy-looking fungi, watching the rush of the water and the willow leaves zipping past us like acid-lemon fish.

The level of the river is high when we reach Dedham, almost threatening to wash over its banks. A giant infinity pool that merges with the green sweep of the water meadow to the left.

The mill here looks severe on the river; its charm has been washed away by development, leaving it too jet-washed clean, too neat. All rude red brick and modern glass against the sleepiness and oldness of the water, it is a civilised barrier to our escape. We continue on our way.

The water is so soft that the paddles hardly seem to make any difference. It's like pushing against whipped air. In summer this part of the river is thick with rowing boats heading to and from Flatford. Now, at the end of the season, there are just two or three careering upstream, pinballing off the banks as they make their way back to the hire company in Dedham. They wave at us, brothers in arms. It reminds me of being on holiday in France as a child – our first time abroad as a family – and how my dad insisted on beeping enthusiastically at every other car with a GB sticker.

Ridiculously, I also can't help but feel a bit annoyed, as if the romance of our adventure has somehow been compromised. My fanciful notion of solipsistic exploration exploded. We haven't quite shaken off the last vestiges of society yet. Stevenson experienced a similar frustration during his trip. On the quiet upper Oise he and Simpson had been 'strange and picturesque intruders; and out of people's wonder sprang a sort of light and passing intimacy all along our route'. But after meeting pleasure boats at L'Isle Adam, he complained: 'there was nothing to distinguish the true voyager from the amateur, except, perhaps the filthy condition of my sail,' adding: 'The company in one boat actually thought they recognised me for a neighbour. Was there anything more wounding?'

We have company on the banks too. Two cyclists and bands of cagoule-shrouded walkers match the rhythm of the Pipe's beaver-tailed paddles with their own Gore-Tex and lycra swish. The water is high, almost level with the meadows, and their conversations skim over it like flattened stones. Talk of dinner menus, doctor appointments, TV choices, sore arses, all bounce over to the canoe before sinking into the river, grey-ing in the afternoon's dying light, to be swept away to the next frothing lock.

The river swings left and right, like it's trying to shake the walkers from its banks. There's no sign of the heron or of kingfisher, just meadows studded with the elephant legs of old pollards, bollings like arthritic knuckles marking the path of the woodman's saw. There's also no sight of the cattle that graze this land, although the fields and banks have been punched into a mess of mud – in many places the cows have left casts of their lower legs to harden slowly in the cool autumn air. Some parts of the bank have been trampled so low that the river is making its own bid for freedom, a slow, swampy trickle back to the old routes it probably hasn't wetted since Saxon times. The river still remembers.

The number of people swelled as we got closer to Flatford, a fitting name for the flattest of land and flattest of rivers. But, having passed through the heart of Constable country, the land of *The Hay Wain*, the jewel in the crown of the Dedham Vale AONB, the river regains its wildness. We have finally escaped.

The trees seem as if they are leaning towards the water, cloaking it, forming a protective mantle with their soughing branches. It feels older, less managed, less contained here; there is also a strangeness to the place. Perhaps it is the slow transition between worlds, or maybe it is the gothic gloom; but I can't help but think of the creature that was once said to haunt this river: the Bures dragon, the serpent of the Stour.

I imagine its crested head and saw teeth, the thrash of its humped body in the water almost drowning out the screams of horror of the men who have been called on to kill it: who have seen the savaged body of the shepherd and a field emptied of sheep. A description of the most famous encounter, dated at 1405 and credited to Monk John de Trokelowe, states that arrows 'bounced off his back if it were iron or hard rock'. One explanation for the creature was that it was an escaped crocodile, brought back from the Crusades to the Tower of London for Richard I. If so, its freedom was not to last long; it is said this beast was killed by Sir George Marney, an event depicted in the stained-glass window at Wormingford church.

On the left bank the trees are thick, knitted together by a bristling wall of scrub and nettles with barbs like glass needles. I imagine it is mazed with small paths too, where deer, badger and fox have barged and picked their way through, browsing on woody shoots and the last of the year's berries. We camped somewhere similar last night, holed up like outlaws, jumping at every muntjac bark and reduced to nervous silence by the wandering yellow light of a torch beam. Escaping from society can be exhilarating, but it can also be pretty unnerving.

Here, though, the woodland is too wet to camp. We carry on, looking for a more promising site, but as the light slips away the rain starts. Soft splodges burst like wet balloons on the canoe. It feels like the sky is getting ready to really let go. We wanted to reach the start of the estuary by nightfall, but now we need to stop. Getting drenched before spending a night outside would be a disaster.

Both of us are quiet. These adventures, these river escapes are not all bright water and endless sun. As well as the hard slog of paddling and disputes over river access, camping can be quite the challenge. Wild camping is not allowed (unlike in Scotland). Even if we can find somewhere hidden from view, the chances are it could be soggy, freezing and uncomfortable.

Eventually we stop by the right bank. It's a beautiful spot. Facing away from the stretch of river we have been travelling along, the southern leg of the Stour bows out in front, a stomach-shaped loop that curves softly out of view; the water is a deeper, richer black than the charcoal greys of the land. Beyond that, swags of orange lights mark the train line, swinging in the damp breeze like wreckers' lamps.

Unable to find any suitable trees, we decide to make use of a nearby metal fence that forms part of a cattle-free corral, lashing the hammocks to steel struts and gates. We get the tarps up just as the heavens finally open, the wind pulling at the ropes and turning the canvas canopy into a sodden parachute.

We are both crouching round the stove, heating soup and making tea, when the birds arrive. Lapwings fall from the sky like helicoptering sycamore seeds, tumbling on paddle wings with a *te-wit te-wit* screech that knifes through the gusting wind. We watch open-mouthed as more and more come, the white of their wings flashing in the gloom as they flop towards the black water to our right. I love lapwings. The sheer jestering, jinking craziness of them. Chaucer said the lapwing was false, 'ful of treacherye', and the collective noun for them is a deceit, earned perhaps by their strategy of feigning injury to lure predators away from the nest. Paul Evans, in his beautiful *Field Notes From the Edge*, says that lapwings also feign madness, 'mobbing intruders ... [their] mock insanity masking a calculated communal mind'.

Other birds follow; we can't see them in the gloom but we can hear them. The water-ski landings, the squabbling cries and the whomping beat of slowing wings. It is the rhythm of the day fading into the stillness of night.

Wriggling into a sleeping bag in a hammock is surprisingly difficult. Every squirm and fidget does nothing but leave me balled up and uncomfortable, my sleeping bag reduced to an extravagant ankle warmer. I try a different tack, getting out to step into the bag before tumbling into the hammock like a cut log. I angle myself so I can see the slow white eye of the moon, bright through a small gap in the clouds, reflecting off the surface of the river to my left. As a child I used to be able to name dozens of the moon's landmarks – the Sea of Serenity, the Sea of Tranquility, the Sea of Crises and the Sea of Fecundity – but there are others that have gone, out of memory's reach. I wrap my blanket round my head and bend my knees towards my stomach, breathing hard, enjoying the sensation of warm air puffing into my sleeping bag. I flex my chilled toes and remember one more. The Sea of Cold.

The car-engine hum starts around three. A whir and a crank of bird noise, the occasional laughing duck answered by fluting tweets that swirl out of the throbbing mass; a hodge-podge of shifting, stretching, flumping wings and morning swims in black water too freezing to even think about. The fork of the river is lit by the moon, which has continued its race across the sky, and the orange flare of Manningtree in the distance. Two other phosphorous blooms, doming on the horizon, mark out Ipswich and perhaps Colchester? Or is it Harwich?

I feel too cold to think straight. Without the cloud the temperature has dropped even lower. I huff again into my sleeping bag. Everything feels damp. I try to think of something else, but my teeth are starting to chatter. Above me I can see the cold sparks of the stars. I try to imagine their scorching surfaces, of 7,000°C of heat travelling through space, burning past dust, ice, gas, planets and satellites to warm my shivering bones. I poke my hands out of the sleeping bag and reach towards them. Star-bathing. It'll never catch on.

When I wake again it is almost light and a mist has fallen. It is low enough to drag fleecy-soft on the trees and bushes and blots out everything apart from James's legs as he stands brushing his teeth by the river's edge. I rub the sleep from my eyes and swing my legs out of my hammock and sleeping bag, searching the grass with my feet for my trainers. The tarp is wringing-wet and I can feel the moisture bleeding onto the back of my sweatshirt and neck as I brush against it to tie my laces.

I leave James hunting around in the dry bags with a torch for the tea while I walk down the river to a quiet wooded spot. I secretly dread the call of nature in the wild, and it is a trial: a series of clumsy yogic braces against trees and unexpected stinging nettles. But there is also something amazingly peaceful about al fresco toileting, a heightened sense of your surroundings, which comes with the vulnerability of being in the wilds with your pants down.

I'm pulling up my trousers when I hear a voice.

'Looking for carp?' A shadow is moving out of the swirling mist, a wraith in a peaked cap, a dark shape resting on the crook of an arm. It seems we're never really that far from civilisation after all. The figure comes closer. A man head to toe in camouflage, holding a short fishing rod and a keep net, its mesh webbed with water. He rubs an arm across his face, the stubble rasping on the sleeve of his jacket like sandpaper. I panic.

'No, pike.'

He seems pleased with the response.

'Ah! It's a great spot for pike here. Any luck?'

'No,' I mumble, starting to walk back to camp, 'not yet.'

He's incredulous. His flat vowels slap the air.

'What?! You can't move for 'em here,' he says, falling in step with me.

James's eyes widen when he sees I'm not alone. I wonder if he thinks it's a bailiff or a landowner keen to get us off the land. The fisherman breaks off from talking about lures to jab an accusing finger towards him, hooking the gnarled digit into an arthritic trigger finger.

'You would have been dead if we were in the army, son; I saw your torch a mile away.'

This river is this fisherman's favourite hunting ground. He regularly stomps along both sides of the privately owned banks and onto the neighbouring RSPB reserve to spin for pike. But I'm not sure if it's the fishing or the game of cat-and-mouse he enjoys more – he regales us with tales of repeated confrontations with reserve wardens, bailiffs, landowners and 'fucking kayakers' ruining his fishing. He grins through nicotine-stained teeth.

'I thought I'd get here early this morning, when all the buggers are still in bed.'

He takes a greasy-looking roll-up from behind his ear, lights up and points upstream.

'I'm going to try up there before it gets too light. I'll come back in a bit and show you boys how it's done. Can't believe you haven't caught anything.'

He starts to move off.

'You should stop pissing around and put a line in the water before it gets too light.'

He clambers over a gate and disappears, the red ember of his fag a tiny floating beacon in the mist. We stand in silence before James looks over his mug at me, eyebrows raised.

'I told him we were fishing. I panicked and wanted him to like us,' I explain.

We pack at speed, keen to be back on the water before he returns and discovers that we are bereft of fishing gear and are, in fact, just 'canoe wankers'.

∾

We arrive at Cattawade before 9 a.m., paddling through mist that peels away from water like skin from an orange. For the 'Sudbury to the Sea' pioneers, this marks the end of their patrol, the point where the blue line of the Stour is severed by the tidal barrage and sea wall. Here there is no gradual meeting of currents, no magical place where the water binds together. The edgeland of the river butts up against brutish concrete edge.

A fisherman, hunkered down under a green umbrella, raises his hand in silent greeting from the right bank as we approach the slipway. He watches as we drag the Pipe up the ramp, paint from her bottom leaving a childish crayon scrawl on the mammoth tooth ridges of the concrete. We clump up the slope and over the road to another slipway, this one leading down to the wide mouth of the estuary proper, putting down the canoe to blow on our freezing hands.

We needn't have rushed. There is hardly any water at all. It is a savannah of quivering, moussey mud. Glistening gloop that stretches towards the railway bridge in the distance. Six or seven boats list on their sides like huge open clams, their insides gleaming as if picked clean by gulls. James has been edging down the slope towards the mud and attempts a couple of footsteps before giving up – suckering back towards me and kicking off the sulphurous sludge that is sticking to his legs and riming his trainers.

There is no choice but to wait. We upend the Pipe under the shadow of leylandii that skirt the slipway just as the rain comes; first a few soft drops and then harder, a cold, slicing downpour that burns our faces like hot wire. I root around in my pack for the bright-purple poncho my wife packed for me and I insisted I definitely wouldn't wear.

We sit and watch the fisherman pull in tiddler after tiddler.

'Do you think he knows that there's not going to be any water for hours?' I ask James. 'I bet he's having a good chuckle about it.'

James looks down at his stinking shoes, gazes across at the angler then back at me, my poncho snickering theatrically behind me.

'I expect he is.'

In two hours the water appears almost out of nowhere. It creeps round the sides of the boats and begins to lift and wobble the buoys like giant fishing floats. An egret poking about in the mud is our dipstick, demonstrating the increasing depth with skinny legs. There is a clear route of shallow water that snakes away from the barrage and under the bridge. We drag the Pipe across the road and onto the slipway, aiming her nose at a clear patch of mud between jagged slices of rock. We cling to her sides, using her to keep upright as we totter down the slope, our feet going from under us two or three times. After ten minutes of swearing the front end of the canoe is in the water. James jumps from a rock and straddles her stern, shuffling forward on his knees, bum in the air. He plonks himself down in the seat and shouts at me to follow.

I look at him and the mud, now grooved from the Pipe's keel, James's footprints deep and folding.

'Can't we wait a bit? We could have another cup of tea . . . or a sausage?'

He shoots me a look. I sigh and tiptoe towards the slimy end of the concrete slipway. Paddle in hand, I prance onto one of the rocks, feeling the grip of my trainers skidding down towards the mud.

'Jump!' James shouts, and I leap in a poncho flap, landing face-down in the back of the canoe and smearing large dollops of mud all over my seat. I twist and turn as James levers the paddles into the estuarine gloop, pushing the rest of the canoe towards the water. With a final defiant fart, the Pipe breaks free from the mud and spins out into the widening channel. James is jubilant.

'We're doing it, we're doing it!'

The current is strong, the incoming tide riffling over the shallows and pushing us away from the deeper channel where our paddles can make clean strokes. The rain has lifted but the wind is blowing with the tide and it takes ten minutes to cover the small distance to the railway bridge. Away to the right, a cluster of yachts are still on their side, their keels knifing into water only inches deep. Nearby, on a spit of exposed mudbank, sit thirty or forty cormorants hunched together like sinister penguins, some holding ragged wings to the wind in taxidermic poses.

We are now on the estuary proper and the wind is really buffeting us. We aim for a pink house on the left bank with the intention of hugging the coast all the way round to where the River Orwell pours into the sea. But soon we're sucked back into the middle, and the sound of the waves on wood is like an open-handed slap. We try to turn but there's the very real possibility that if the swell catches us broadside we could go over.

For the first time in the canoe I am terrified. Scared to my bones. It feels like an abrupt change, a mood shift in the water. The river transforming from calm and bosky-banked to sea-wide and rough. This is no longer a gentle quest to shake off the shackles of society. We have now properly ventured beyond the bounds – and safety – of civilisation. And out here it no longer seems like freedom; it feels dangerous.

It's a wake-up call. The language of exploration is traditionally one of dominion and I curse myself for falling into that trap. For thinking that this was all here just for me. That river country is my country. For losing sight of what it is that makes all of this so special: the ceaseless, unstoppable power of it all, the fact that the river doesn't care if it is running over rocks, wood, mud or flesh. To cap it all my sea legs have again failed to appear, and the combination of wind and tide that sends the Pipe wallowing into briny trough after briny trough is making me feel increasingly sick.

James has gone quiet. I assume he's feeling the same. He stops paddling and turns to me, his face creased in smiles.

'This is amazing, oh my God, it's such fun!'

He scrabbles in his bag, his movement and lack of paddling exposing the Pipe to the choppy brown water that rushes at the canoe and foams over its nose. He sits back up while I stare grimly at the horizon, trying to stifle another wave of nausea.

'Selfie!' he shouts against the wind, standing in the rocking nose of the canoe, his phone outstretched.

The conditions go from bad to worse, and even James admits we should try to head for the side again, to get out of the wind that is now creaming the tips of the waves. For forty-five minutes we paddle hard but hardly move. The converted maltings at Mistley are a gentrified middle finger to our progress. We face the waves at an angle, the current and the wind constantly grabbing the Pipe by the nose, trying to twist her and pull her in a different direction.

Closer to land the situation doesn't improve. Although we are out of the wind, the current from the rushing tide is desperate to pour itself over the salt marsh on the west bank. We are powerless to stop it and within a couple of minutes have been wedged against drifts of estuary mud, with the waves battering the side, pinning us in position and threatening to dump us out of the Pipe, which creaks in protest. A stuck pig. There's no way we can fight back out onto the water so instead we try to land. James takes off his shoes and socks and sinks in up to his knees, gamely heaving the Pipe onto more solid parts of mud. He offers me a hand and I jump for a mat of reeds, land and take several paces forward, leaving my trainers behind in deep folds of beige and black mud. The pair of us heave the canoe onto the firmest patch of ground we can find and stand there, considering our position. We couldn't have landed in a worse place: we are miles from anywhere, surrounded by quaking mud and salt marsh that is quickly disappearing under sheets of water.

James stays with the canoe while I retrieve my sodden trainers and walk off to see if there is a road nearby. The path winds round the estuary; there is inundated salt marsh to my right and a mix of freshwater marsh and reclaimed farmland to the left. I spot a figure up in front of me, the first person I have seen on this walkway. I hurry towards him, hoping he has just emerged from some easily accessible car park.

He hasn't and is trying his hardest to ignore me.

'Morning!' I say brightly, squelching to a stop.

'Hello,' he replies quietly, taking his eye away from a monocular resting on a tripod.

'We've been marooned and we're looking for a road.'

He squints at me and scratches his white beard.

'It's some way,' he says in a Suffolk burr, 'you've got a good two miles to get to the rail track.'

'What about this way?' I ask, pointing behind him.

'Nope,' he says with a flat finality. 'There's farm tracks, but it's another good mile before you hit a road.'

He turns back to his monocular and gazes out over the estuary. I'm not sure if this is the end of the conversation and move from foot to foot, feeling the water rise up round my toes as my weight shifts.

'OK, then,' I say, 'well . . . erm . . . thanks . .' I turn to leave with a dramatic crack of my poncho. It looks like we won't be able to walk out of this one. I've only gone about ten feet when he calls out.

'Hang on.'

I turn hopefully, thinking that he is going to suggest an alternative solution.

'Yes?'

'Try not to scare the birds will you.'

James has put the stove on by the time I get back to the Pipe and looks unconcerned by the situation. The water has clearly risen and the network of mudflats has completely disappeared. We drink tea quietly, looking at the buildings of Mistley and Manningtree over the other side of the estuary, and decide that attempting the 1,000-yard crossing is pretty much our only option.

The waves are still coming in fast when we climb back into the boat, but the venom of the wind seems to have gone, the sting of the turning tide having been drawn by the mud. We stick our paddles down into the gloop and rock back and forth, inching the Pipe forward, trying to free her from her muddy berth. The current grabs the nose of the canoe, the ebb still hard, and she creaks in protest. We strike again and again, splashes of water and liquid mud covering our arms and

backs, before squirting forward and bumping into sharp, rushing waves. We paddle harder than we've ever paddled before
– probably inefficiently deep – trying to lever ourselves out
onto the deeper channel. At first we are somehow in tune with
the water, our strokes jumping the canoe from wave to wave.
We pause to try and re-angle the nose of the Pipe towards the
beach on the other side and we lose our rhythm, paddling into
troughs and causing sheets of greasy water to slide over the
port side and bow. The terror rises in me again. We've nearly
reached the first orange buoy that signals the deepest channel;
I think of the estuary's whirling current and how easy it would
be to get sucked in and bounced under by the water.

We dig deep again; my hands and arms are now burning.
I find myself shouting, 'Pull! Pull!' like the desperate captain of
a whaling boat, my words swallowed by the wind. We reach a
second buoy and the water releases us. Maybe it is the arrival of
the slack tide, or perhaps the shelter of the land, but the waves
are gone. I can easily understand why there are so many old
stories about monsters and serpents lurking in rivers, estuaries
and seas. With the change of current it's hard not to imagine
intent – to give the tidal pulses and humped waves anthropo-
morphic qualities. Whatever force is on our side, natural or
supernatural, we don't stop until we reach the beach, where we
collapse out of the boat and embrace. The adrenaline is shuddering through my system and I've never been so happy to feel
the ground beneath my feet.

We get out the stove and plonk ourselves down on the Pipe's wooden seats to eat soup and wait for a lift back to our car.

'Did you really enjoy that?' I ask James. He pauses between mouthfuls, blowing on his spoon.

'God yes,' he says, 'it was amazing. You know – to feel like we were really battling and with all the spray and water coming over us.'

'But weren't you scared?'

'Nah, although . . .' he pauses.

'What?'

'I did have a slight concern that the Pipe might just split in two. You know, she's home-made so there's always a worry.'

He eats his last bit of bread and lies back contentedly, putting his head on a rucksack and his feet on the central seat of the canoe. I stare at him, the horror of his words slowly sinking in.

'And did you worry about that before or after the selfie?'

There has been a frost, the first of the year. It furs the car, dusts leaves with iron filings of ice and scribbles across the bottom of the Pipe as she lies beached in the garden, leaving a snail-trail of cold that blends with the scratches and scrapes collected from her river adventures. Her battle scars. We slide her over to the car and perform a knee-trembling snatch-lift onto the roof rack before wiping wet hands on trousers and checking our gear. Paddles. Buoyancy aids. Thermos. Boiled eggs.

It's a good hour's drive to Aldeburgh and the starting point of today's trip. James has been pushing to do another estuary after the Stour and, although I'm apprehensive of rough water and rough weather, I am drawn to the idea of exploring another edgeland, a place where river turns to sea, where salt water meets fresh. Another secret window, where the river grows too wide to be spanned by bridges, where the start of water and the end of land is slippery and hard to define.

But we have learnt our lessons from the Stour, scalded as we were by the power of the tide that stranded us on mudflats, threatened to shake the Pipe apart and put us in the drink. My friend Giles, who knows that stretch of water well, assured me such an incident would have left us 'properly dead'. Today, rather than fighting the currents and the rushing tide, we will attempt to go with it, following the sea's trembling rush upstream as it creeps and pours over mudflats and salt marsh, before being sucked out again by the turning tide.

We arrive at Aldeburgh an hour after low tide, the slack water already gathering for another push inland. To our left the Martello Tower sticks up like a half-built sandcastle between the Alde and the North Sea, the largest and most northerly of a chain of towers built to stop Napoleon. Beyond that, on the widening spit of land that noses into the North Sea, is the Orford Ness National Nature Reserve. A former Atomic Weapons Research Establishment, its wind-and salt-blasted buildings now look out on a fragile beauty: 2,000 acres of grazing marsh, reed marsh, brackish lagoons and vegetated shingle supporting hundreds of rare species. We unload, half-carrying, half-skidding the Pipe down the yacht club's seaweed-fringed slipway, eager to get underway. The knocking masts of the boats, dry-docked for winter, ring out loud in a gin-clear sky. A lone man works on one of them, sanding down a hull calloused with barnacles, his radio tootling and burbling.

We head out straight, the canoe's nose pointing towards the river's first bend. The wind, the first taste of a storm that is forecast to hit tomorrow, funnels down the seaward stretch of the Alde and forces lumps of water under the Pipe. They hit hard, like speed bumps.

The Alde is comparatively short, with less than 20 miles separating its source in Laxfield (close to where Suffolk's Blyth also bubbles into life) and its mouth near Orford, where it becomes known as the Ore. Yet in some ways it feels like the biggest river we have explored so far. As we paddle into the winter sun, the whole horizon shimmers. The water, the acres of mud, the beaches and soggy spits all gleam, all ripple with light. It's hard to tell where the river stops and the land begins.

With the tide still not completely with us we decide to take a break and allow the water to gather. We get the Pipe up to what James calls 'ramming speed' and beach ourselves on a shingle spit that spears out into the water. But these are no stones. It is a mass of shellfish and crab, a great, grey beach of shells, clam and carapace; a huge graveyard of mussels, spattered with barnacles and mud. It's impossible to stand in any one place for long without sinking down to the ankles, so we drink our tea on the move, taking crunching steps round tiny blue lagoons of trapped water. James, stomping theatrically over a pile of broken shell, says it reminds him of a grisly scene from *Terminator 2* in which robotic feet smash through the burnt remains of human skulls.

'It's like,' he says, waving a disembodied crab claw at me, 'we're at the end of the world.' I know what he means; there is a sense of loneliness here, that we've escaped to a place where both land and time are running out.

We collect shells to avoid thinking about the bone-chilling cold, arranging them on the nose of the Pipe as the water begins to rise around us, the shallow pools widening into each other. A gull, disturbed by our presence, reluctantly throws itself into the wind. The shell spit is now less solid than ever, a wavering hazy line between land and water. Within minutes we can actually see the tide. While the river flows seaward, the current piles against it and over it, leaving the surface of the water taut, occasionally breaking into an angry swirl, or rising into sharp spikes like the black dorsal fins of hundreds of fish jostling to get upstream. It is also a clear sign for us to get going. I clamber back in and James pushes off, jumping onto the Pipe as she glides away from the mussel island and back into the river.

There are plenty of boats here, but no one to sail them. We try to guess the names painted on their sides before we reach their mooring buoys, disappointed that close up 'Witches Spank' becomes 'Vital Spark', the 'Onion' the slightly more cosmic 'Orion'. I think of my five-year-old daughter's announcement a couple of months ago while taking a river taxi in Beccles: 'If I had a boat I'd call it the Idi-yacht.'

As the boats thin out, the number of birds increases and we find ourselves relying on them to navigate the narrow channels through the mud: the throngs of feeding waders mark the waterline, galloping away in startled herds when the canoe gets too close.

Even with the tide's help it takes more than an hour to reach Iken, but we couldn't have asked for a better day. The sky is a cold blue, fading to milk at the edges; clear apart from a single vapour trail, stretched and pulled by the wind into a ragged backbone of fluffy vertebrae. There are clouds of a different sort too. Dunlin. Only visible when the sun hits their white chests and the underside of their whirring wings, they pulse and rush above the water. Their feathers glint like the flashing scales of silver fish with each dip and turn. We stop paddling to watch, but their murmuration finishes as quickly as it began, the birds dropping like beautiful pebbles onto a curve of mud near the right bank, rooting their bills in the gloop.

Alde Mudflats stretches for almost three miles around the church that overlooks the estuary, emerging with each low tide. An Atlantis of nutritious, invertebrate-filled mud. Leased from the Crown Estate by Suffolk Wildlife Trust, it is a nature reserve, a refuge for a huge number of birds. In fact, I don't think I've ever seen so many in one place. Curlew stilt-walk across the mud, their bills a needle-thin shoehorn of bone-hard keratin, prodding and searching. Others take off as we near, like feathered Concordes with skinny nose cones lowered. Further away there are avocet, oystercatchers, redshank and many others I cannot name. I feel a slight sense of frustration at not knowing them, at not being able to separate and identify the mass of whimpering, mournful cries that wobble out over the estuary.

But in some ways it doesn't matter. Part of what I find amazing about experiencing nature are those moments of wild chaos, the pure clamour of life when nature and self are suddenly wrapped up together in one song. The boundlessness of the natural world doesn't just surround me or impress me; it assimilates me, claims me as its own. The experience is often fleeting, but it is undeniably precious. Soul-nourishingly so. What's more, I can feel it here on this estuary. For haunting seconds, in the thrum of beating wings, the creeping water and the power of the rushing tide, I become gloriously, precariously, part of it.

The tide is hurrying ahead of us now. We're on a Nantucket sleigh ride powered by the great brown flukes of water rushing inland. The paddling is so easy that we shoot past the point where we planned to turn round, gliding on towards the reed-lined banks that lead to Snape Maltings, which appears like a great ship ghosting above the water.

The sun is beginning to set as we decide to head back and the waterscape has now completely transformed. The mudbanks and tortuous channels we navigated on the way in have disappeared, smoothed away by water. Sinuous bends are replaced with a wideness that is both awe-inspiring and confusing. The submerged mud continues to do strange things to the current: the now retreating water swirls and thuds under the canoe, pushing the nose first one way and then the other. We head for where the water is deepest, a path marked by drowned trees, their tallest salt-blasted branches topped by plastic milk bottles covered in blistered red paint.

I wonder how the trees came to be here. It feels eerie; like we are paddling over a drowned landscape. It's as if there could be whole villages or towns beneath us, fields and playgrounds swamped, church bells clanking silently with the pull of the tide, the legion dead gazing with hollow eyes at the Pipe's scarred bottom. It reminds me of Dunwich just a few minutes away, the formerly prosperous Suffolk port that went from rotten borough to capital of Doggerland. A slow, sad slip into the sea.

The light is going more quickly than the water, draining out from behind us, the last rays sucked down into the murky estuary. From behind us comes a cicada shriek and the whirring hum of hundreds of wings. We duck instinctively. It is the dunlin again. Wave after wave of them, shooting over us, heading for land and for roost. We snap on our head torches, the beams search-lighting out across the open water. We follow the trail of the dunlin and the winking orange light from Orford Ness, towards the car and home.

The surface is thick with silt, a hot-chocolate skin; tiny motes of floating land swirl with each paddle stroke, sticking to our beaver-tailed blades and riming the sides of the canoe. The river is land in waiting. Our trips down the Stour and here in this estuary have been liberating experiences in many ways: the realisation that even on busier rivers it is still possible to slip from the well-trod to the wild; the intensity of being in those edgelands between land and sea; perhaps even the way in which the danger itself elicits moments of appreciation – when life, death and every wet wonder burns bright like a rare but beautiful comet. I've relished the freedom of the river, and though I'm ready to return home to warm feet and hands, now so painfully pinched by the cold, in my head I'm already planning our next escape.

CHAPTER 3

Abuse and misuse

The Christmas decorations are still up when we head to the Lark. It is early morning but the car park at Tesco is already filling up with shoppers eager to restock their festive rations and plug the yawning gap between Christmas and New Year. As we start to unload the canoe I watch them moving from car to shop and back without even glancing down at the river. And why should they? It is almost unbearably ugly. Penned with steel fences and tarmac, trammelled through a flat-bottomed wedge of slimy concrete, it is a sight that left Roger Deakin crying in his car and other conservationists asking how something so hideous could ever have been allowed. I've heard it said that Tesco actually wanted to hide the whole river, but in the end opposition from planners and locals persuaded them to give it concrete wellies rather than bury it alive.

I think I probably lived in Bury St Edmunds for a good year

before I even noticed the river. Before I realised that the sludge-filled ditch where I went running was the Linnet, a tributary of the Lark. The Lark. The clue is in the name. A place that should sing and burble in flight. One of only 200 chalk streams in the world, it ought to be revered and loved, not subdued with concrete, broken by sluices and cruel flood defences. It is a source of shame, or bloody well ought to be.

Of course, along with development, abstraction (removing water from the ground source) has played its part too. Bury St Edmunds: Sugar Town. The Silver Spoon factory sucks up vast quantities of water, as does Greene King to produce its pale ale, while agriculture and the expanding population use up gallon after precious gallon, leaving the river drained and sickened.

I have been warned off trying to canoe here. The fishing club downstream that has worked with Suffolk Wildlife Trust to restore the waterway didn't want us to disturb the fish, while canoeists expressed doubts about whether it could be paddled, and why would we want to anyway? 'It is', they said, 'a ditch.' But it is our ditch. The idea of exploring somewhere so close to home, yet so unknown, is massively appealing. There are stretches where it can be walked, thanks to a hard-fought campaign by the Bury Water Meadows Group to reinstate footpaths, but there's so much more to rivers. I want to feel its water. And so we plan to spend two days following the Lark's course from Tesco in Bury, through the Brecks and the Fens to its outpouring into the Great Ouse.

At the far end of the car park we see-saw the Pipe over the fence and throw our gear after it onto a shingle-filled honeycomb of plastic, dotted with a few young trees that look as if they're in the process of giving up the ghost. Up close, the concrete wedge is even more depressing. A few inches of murky water dribbles over a slimy lip down to muck-covered stones. Looking upstream, the river really is boxed in: separated from its floodplain and starved of any of the natural processes that could elevate it above a giant car-park puddle.

The water isn't high enough to paddle so we set off at a walk, a slow sloshing stomp through the river: through upturned bottles, past polystyrene takeaway shells, smashed hubcaps, rusting gas canisters and dozens of footballs, slowly turning in the current. It's such a shame to see how bad the littering is here. But it is by no means a problem restricted to the Lark. Neglect threatens rivers across Britain, discarded items, particularly plastic, becoming a regular, if unwelcome, part of the scenery and posing a serious threat to the rivers' wildlife.

Litter has always been an issue for rivers; there is no statutory duty on aquatic litter. And water, which is so brilliant at collecting rubbish, refuses to let the wind-blown, the carelessly dropped and the drunkenly thrown slide through its liquid grip. Instead litter is sucked, pulled and tumbled by the current, not digested, but broken down into a vast soup of microplastics that remain in the river or wash into the sea. Countrywide, an annual tide of eight million tonnes of plastic is thought to end up in the sea, to be eaten by fish, then bigger fish, then us. One study by scientists at Ghent University suggests that seafood lovers could be consuming up to 11,000 pieces of plastic each year.

Out of sight of Tesco is a bridge I've never seen before; at least not in the flesh. I recognise it from a black and white picture taken in the late nineteenth century, a time when barges used to float their way down from the Ouse, when this river was not a trickle but a wide expanse of water. A coal road. Behind us, where the car park is now, was St Saviour's Wharf, a place once busy with trade. It's tempting to think of these times as the glory days of the river, but in reality its treatment was just as destructive. The banks were pushed out to twice, three times their natural width, without any thought as to what that would do to this ecosystem. Hello navigable channel, farewell natural processes. The flow of the river was lost, removing the conveyer-belt current, the life. Another footnote of abuse.

The bridge's arch is huge, some 20 feet up and at least that wide; an impressive piece of engineering. We walk slowly, pushing the Pipe in front, into the first stretch of the river that cannot be seen from public land. A solitary kingfisher appears, making a hummingbird buzz as it flies from perch to perch; from twisted wires to foul-smelling outflow pipe; from broken fence to shopping trolley. The river begins to vary in depth, from ankle-deep to potholes of stinking silt that send us stumbling towards the bank. The gentle trickle of the water is a sad song of neglect.

The first mile is more walking than paddling. We rarely manage ten strokes before the Pipe grumbles along the bed of the river. The current is stronger, though, where the river has reverted back to a more natural width: a pulsing gush that presses our legs as we tramp along, sending the Pipe dancing ahead of us on its rope like an excited dog.

The concrete entrance to Tollgate Bridge is guarded by another shopping trolley, wire ribs fleshed with a greying mesh of river-woven weed, sticks and mud. A sign, advertising an offer long since gone, hangs from a single rusting rivet. I walk carefully, avoiding flints, pipes and bottles, all mole-furred with a brown algal slime that softens their edges, like the coral-covered remains of sunken boats. Up ahead we spot a bathtub, upside down, its fibreglass bottom dented and cracked, malformed and fallen, like a badly baked loaf. But up close it seems that the local otters have accepted it as part of their territory. Along its back edge sit three or four spraints, grey like ash and flaked with scales. I can see hair-thin fish ribs and necklace strings of vertebrae. There are bigger remains too. A signal crayfish. An emptied-out husk, wolfed down by a hungry otter. I imagine him chanking on it, the crunch of his teeth on armoured carapace. A cat-like chew. A beautiful wet-whiskered troll under this busy town bridge.

I'm surprised to find otters here, but hugely pleased. Despite all the rubbish, the water is clean enough for them. The twentieth century was a tough time for the otter: persecuted, poisoned by pesticides and made homeless through the destruction of wetlands, an animal that was once widespread was pushed to the brink of extinction. But following the banning of a range of pesticides, including the now notorious DDT, and efforts to improve water quality and riparian habitats, the otter is back. And there is a long history of otters being in and around this spot before. Records show that in 1903, when the river was effectively canalised but still thick with eels and fish, hunters from Essex met at this bridge and sent hounds upstream. At Lackford Bridge they caught a dog otter weighing 'some 24 pounds'. It is hard to think of a sadder and more pointless trophy. I guess it makes the indignity of shitting on a bath seem like wonderful progress.

I've lost my bearings slightly. I'm not quite sure where we are. My knowledge of the land is as useful on the river as a Tube map is for walking across London. My guess is we're near Fornham, a settlement with a Saxon pedigree that loosely means something like 'homestead by the trout stream'. There's little sign of fish, though. Just more rubbish: polystyrene cases, a TV and three or four footballs, bobbing along like dumplings in stew.

We can hear the sound of rushing water and expect another weir. But, rounding the bend, we can see a pipe, an arm's span wide, emptying frothing water into the river. This is a sewage outflow – or, as water companies have tried to rebrand them, 'the water recycling outflow' – where treated waste water is returned to source. These kinds of pipes have been a common sighting on all the rivers we've been on. But their outpourings aren't always so innocent. Analysis by the World Wide Fund for Nature (WWF) in 2017 suggested that raw sewage is flowing into rivers at thousands of sites in England and Wales. The report said that only 14 per cent of rivers in England have a good ecological status, compared with 27 per cent in 2010. A total of 40 per cent of England and Wales's rivers were reported to be polluted with sewage, pumped from 18,000 outflow sites operated by water companies. Along with the sewage come antidepressants, birth-control hormones, other medicines and recreational drugs; all flushed out of our bodies and down the loo.

But on the Lark it is not so much the level of pollution that is the most obvious concern, but the amount of water. Many people who see the surging river close to here assume it is the source, rather than the trickle that wells up six miles away at Bradfield Combust. Chalk streams like the Lark are often winterbournes: they only flow from source to mouth from late autumn to early summer and their beds can become bone-dry in the high summer.

The point at which a chalk stream flows permanently is called the perennial head; it is where the water table never falls below the river bed. Abstraction can cause water levels beneath the earth to fall and perennial heads to move down-stream. In drought years large-scale abstraction has caused some chalk rivers to dry out completely and reduced others to trickles.

Until 1963 there were no legal controls governing water abstraction, and the amount of water removed increased dra-matically during the twentieth century. Today environmental factors are taken into consideration, but still 13 per cent of rivers and 42 per cent of ground-water aquifers in England are considered to be under stress because too much water is being taken away.

The result? Less water, which is often of a poorer quality. On the Lark the amount of water extracted is not sustainable. At the moment the flow in four water bodies on the upper Lark is suitable to sustain invertebrates – a cornerstone of the whole river's ecosystem – for only 67 per cent of the time. The Environment Agency's aim for this part of the river is to see ecology supported for 95 per cent of the time, and Anglian Water is working hard to reduce abstraction, agreeing to reduce the amount of water taken when the flow falls to a certain level at Fornham.

The Lark isn't the only chalk stream that is suffering in this way. Another report, again by the conservation charity WWF, claims that over half of the chalk streams and nearly a quarter of the rivers in England are at risk of drying out, stating that 'Nature and wildlife are losing out in the rush to exploit the planet's water resources. In England and Wales, fewer than one in five rivers are classed as in good ecological health.'

Farmers and anglers have all reported dramatic drops in water levels. Paul Jennings, a farmer and the chairman of the River Chess Association in Buckinghamshire, said that over the last six years the river has been dry 50 per cent of the time, decimating fish populations. The flushes of water that do wet the bed after rainfall are now mainly run-offs from urban or agricultural land that bring silt and pollution with them. Peter King, a project officer from Adur Rivers Trust, Sussex, said that places on the Bevern stream, which used to be swum, can now be walked. Furthermore, as the water ebbs away, interest in rivers falls. The waterway becomes locked into a cycle of neglect.

For the Lark, one option is to re-route upstream the great sewer outpouring in front of us now to flow around or through Bury St Edmunds – at a cost of millions of pounds. The Lark would be invigorated. But there is something unutterably miserable about the idea of restoring this once beautiful and rare chalk stream with the power of flush. It would be the final insult to a river that has been scraped, entombed in concrete and in some ways seemingly forgotten.

The extra water of the outflow causes the canoe to judder as we pass, the current whipping up globs of sticky brown foam that sticks to paddles and takes to the air. A gruesome milkshake froth containing Lord knows what. James has brought a saw to cut through the worst of the blockages – the fallen branches that can't be shifted or bent out of the way – but there are other obstacles too, a mat of debris. Sticks, wrappers, glass bottles and plastic, fishing rods, balls, shoes, flip-flops, boxes, cartons, fridge trays and table legs, all glued together with weed and sludge. Wobbling across it all comes a nappy, ballooned to three times its normal size, like the jelly sail of a Portuguese man o'war. Its other name, the floating terror, seems in this case particularly apt. We ram our way through slowly, pulling ourselves along with overhanging branches or by sticking a leg outside the canoe to kick off from the bank. A precarious Flintstone propulsion.

Another problem affecting our rivers is also clear to see on the Lark. Invasive species. The honeycomb of egg-shaped holes mined into the banks indicates the presence of the American signal crayfish. There is a catacomb here, a labyrinthine lair of muddy tubes that the wash from the canoe and the river's current slaps into, sucking out more silt to cloak what is left of the gravel beds. Eventually, unless action is taken, the banks will collapse completely.

Bigger and brasher than the threatened native white-claw, the American signal is a B-movie monster, a relentless omnivore that will clear the river of food before falling on its own kind. I've heard of whole river beds heaving with them, a Panzer prawn that out-competes its native namesake while delivering a sucker punch of porcelain plague. Their ability to colonise new waterways is second to none. They can walk 1,000 yards a day on pin-pricking legs to fresh hunting grounds, and can last up to three months out of water, while whole colonies have been found perching patiently under bridges waiting for the river level to reveal their hiding holes again.

Those tasked with getting rid of them face an almost impossible task. The Environment Agency encouraged people at a meeting of the Bury Water Meadows Group to obtain licences in order to catch the crayfish on the Lark, and to treat them 'like blackberries' of the river. I spot one as we pull in for lunch, half out of a bank-side hole, pincers hanging down as if they are too heavy to lift, scanning the current with unblinking ball-bearing eyes.

There are signs of other unwelcome visitors. A small cage floating on a raft signals the presence of mink, escaped, rescued and released from fur farms since the 1950s to devastate whole ecosystems. They have been relentlessly hunted ever since, with traps dotting most waterways that I've been on. I've only seen a trapped mink once and it was, to be honest, terrifying. It fizzed and spat like potassium meeting water, a whirling comet of teeth and claw. But I can't help feeling sorry for them – as I did the lumbering coypu, the oversized guinea pigs that once bumbled along the rivers of East Anglia only to be trapped and dispatched. The wrong kind of wild.

The river has opened up by the time we reach the lock at Fornham. The river here is secret and special. The water is low, but deep enough for us to canoe, and it riffles and skids over the

bed, a sucking, chuckling burble. It feels like the Lark is singing again. The strength of the flow increases as the Flempton
stream swings into the Lark. The river bed is more natural here,
full of nodules of flint and gravel. To the left I can make out
the bird hides of Lackford Lakes nature reserves. Dark blocks
against grey, wader-stalked waters.

The water level drops as the river widens and we get out,
splashing through the shallows. I take the centre of the course
while James, in his sodden wellies, sticks close to the left bank.
The mud is surprisingly deep and James slips, his feet sinking
down into the ooze while his hands disappear up to the wrist in
the bank, forming a human bridge. I slosh over to help, putting
my arms round his chest and trying to lift him free. I can feel
my own feet slowly sinking. A cold embrace that creeps over my
ankles and suckers up my shin. I stop pulling him and try to tug
myself clear. My feet move, but the waders stay glued in the mud.

'Oh shit.'

James wriggles and tries to look behind him.

'What? Are you OK?'

'I think I'm stuck too.'

We take a breather. My arms are still locked round James's
waist and my head is resting on his back, his arse jutting into
my lap. He starts laughing.

'You realise this is how they'll find us when they send out
the search party on Monday,' he says. 'Frozen together, with
you mounting me.'

It takes a good five minutes to inch ourselves free, both of us scrambling up to the bank to lie panting on our backs, our legs encased in a stinking, sulphurous gloop.

Not far from the replica Anglo-Saxon village, where ancient knapped arrowheads are still kicked to the surface by digging rabbits, the Bury Trout Club has been turning back the clock. Over the past decade they have been working to transform a stretch of the Lark at West Stow from a straight, dredged channel into a sinuous, bustling river. Reducing the river's width has increased the flow, oxygenating the water and flushing away deposits of silt.

Meanders and riffles have now been reinstated, along with shallows and deep pools, while some 2,500 flowers have been planted along the banks. Trout are already beginning to return and so too has the sound, the slowing and speeding water trilling and singing like the most beautiful bird. The Lark has found its voice. Fish swish upstream in tight formations while more lurk in the calmer, deeper water, waiting for the current to deliver food to gaping mouths. The canoe slips through narrows and round trickling bends to speed over water that licks white over stone and wood. The river project has been described as 'rewilding'. It might sound like a bit of a stretch but I get what they mean; whether it is the re-establishment of temperate rainforest, or the reinstatement of megafauna, sometimes nature needs a helping hand to restore its balance.

What is clear is how quickly water responds. In New Zealand, those behind an effort to recreate the giant kauri forests decimated by European loggers say it will be 350 years before the project has an impact. But water, after just a few years, sometimes even less, will bubble and hum with life, sustaining invertebrates, birds and mammals: a whole ecosystem can be restored within an evolutionary blink. This small patch is a hint of what could be achieved along the whole river.

About a mile, possibly two, from West Stow the river, whether through its own devices or more intervention, is ribbed with tear-drop spits of black stone. The water shoots round them, repeatedly stranding us, forcing us to wade in and push the Pipe back towards a clear channel. The light is fading. The grey day is now greyer. We head for the bank, which is protected from crayfish with logs of birch lashed together with thick wire, and pull the canoe from the water. A small woodland slopes down to a barbed-wire fence that separates us from flooded fields and carr. There are two or three trees close to the fence, a loose triangle that will keep our hammocks well out of sight.

We turn in at eight as the temperature drops, fearful that if we get cold there will be no way back. The sound of the river is truly beautiful, a sleepless lullaby of knocking stones and shushing water. That, combined with the swing of the hammock, takes me under. Dark and dreamless.

In the morning we break camp and I wade into the water to pack the canoe before we get going, easing our way round the shingle banks easily. There is a quiet magic about the first few strokes in a canoe. The quietness of morning is in the water itself. It folds like bed sheets round the paddles. Cotton-soft, whispering and washing over the wood. The tired splashing of last night gone. Knives into liquid butter, the only sound is the drip of the raised blade before it goes under again and pushes on.

Slowly the river narrows until it is no wider than a deer path. Burr reeds and banks hem us in. I also get the sense that the landowner isn't too keen on river access. Logs and wooden signs have been positioned across the river, sometimes even apparently screwed together to create an immovable obstacle. Barbed wire, which usually swags the top of the bank, has been strung right by the water, the steel teeth dragging on our clothes as we inch through. One strand is even tossed across the river's route. What should have been a five-minute stretch takes a good hour of shifting, sweating and pushing. We stop talking at the sound of the tractor. I feel too tired for confrontation, to come face to face with someone who seems to guard the water so savagely. I'm not sure what we'll say. Plead ignorance? Argue grandly that we believe in free access? Our worries come to naught. The 'tractor' is an unmanned engine; a crude diesel-powered pump draining the land, jetting a brownish sludge into the river like a half-hearted water cannon.

We push on. Past the dust and the din of the industrial flour mill at Icklingham, through the concrete barricades near Cavenham and out to where the river is wide, uncluttered and unkinked. We now know there's little chance of reaching the mouth of the Lark today.

We paddle hard and fast, barely resting between strokes. Exhausting ourselves. Overhead the air traffic is increasing. Military planes from the US base at Mildenhall drone overhead every ten minutes or so, the bowel-shaking bass notes of their engines making conversation almost impossible. Gangs of long-tailed tits – bumbarrels – fidget, whistle and click in knots of scrub, their feathers a delicate pink, like red socks in a white wash, under a pied cape. A sheep has fallen into the river, or at least its corpse has. It floats on its back, its ribcage like the bare struts of a half-built boat, ragged strands of fleece bobbing in the current and the wash from the canoe. Most of its face has gone, pecked, nibbled and pinched by scavengers from the air and water. The exposed teeth are fixed in a lunatic grin. One dip too many.

The sluice gates appear soon after. We stop and get out, looking at the great green sheets of water disappearing over an almost vertical drop. The Pipe wouldn't survive the leap and I doubt we would either. The only option is to lug her across the dual carriageway, which, given the speed at which we can carry her, feels like nothing short of a suicide mission.

For now it is the end of the road.

A week later we slide the Pipe back into the water by the Jude's Ferry pub, close to the bridge that marks the start of the Lark's official navigation. The water is shaded by trees and full of ice. It cracks and splits as the canoe's nose hits, opening up a wedge of dark, cold water. We dip paddles, spooning shards of ice up to the surface, and ease our way past two narrowboats that cling to the bank like nervous swimmers.

The river is a world away from the one we left about a mile or so upstream and is now a meandering flow past scrub and woodland. On the right bank a flock of Jacob's sheep watch us before taking flight, galloping across the field like a great mutton locomotive billowing out fleecy puffs of steam behind it.

The day is clear and cold, just a touch above freezing, the sun high and almost painfully bright. The river is absolutely still. With the increased depth all urgency has gone from the water. Green and clean. It is in no rush to get anywhere. James mentions swimming, and it does look inviting. I imagine that breathtaking plunge followed by the pure, cold joy of cutting through the water; the softness of the river matched by the softness of the colours: pond-green water over pink skin. This part of the river used to be known as the Jordan of the Fens. People would come for miles to be baptised here; the river washed them clean, loosed their tongues. Heads that dipped below the cold water emerged reborn. Renewed. The practice continued until the 1970s, when fears were raised about the safety and cleanliness of the water. The holy is no match for health and safety.

Perhaps the most famous baptism to have taken place was that of the preacher Charles Haddon Spurgeon, who was immersed on 3 May 1850. Writing in his autobiography, Spurgeon describes how, just a few weeks before his sixteenth birthday, he walked for eight miles to reach the old chain ferry: 'The wind blew down the river with a cutting blast, as my turn came to wade into the flood; but after I had walked a few steps, and noted the people on the ferry-boat, and in boats, and on either shore, I felt as if Heaven, and earth, and hell, might all gaze upon me; for I was not ashamed, there and then, to own myself a follower of the Lamb. My timidity was washed away; it floated down the river into the sea, and must have been devoured by the fishes, for I have never felt anything of the kind since . . . I lost a thousand fears in that River Lark.'

We hit the ice as the river splits before Isleham, taking the new cut that leads up to the lock past lines of moored barges. It rumbles along the side of the canoe, slowing us to a crawl. The sound is incredible. A low, guttural growl, rising to a full-throated roar as the ice thickens from a crust to more than an inch. The Pipe is an ice-breaker, grinding, crunching through.

When we stop for breath we can hear the ice singing around us. Whistling. Popping. I've read accounts of the groans of glaciers and the ominous creak of pack ice surrounding ships, but I never expected to experience anything like this on the Lark. Our little old Lark; frozen in flight.

James fishes out lumps of ice and holds them up to the sun. Thick windowpanes, occasionally bubbled but clear enough to see through, they lend the trees and the water an eerie coolness. Each time we stop it is harder to start, as though the Pipe is being frozen into place. It has taken us twenty minutes to cover about 50 yards. We thought the ice would just be an isolated patch, a result of shade from the willows and alder; but, looking ahead, it stretches further – all the way to the distant lock. A swan loitering on the bank slips down onto the river, skidding past on black-gummed feet to reach the trail of open water we have left behind us. It waggles its tail and is off.

Perhaps I shouldn't be surprised by the freeze. After all, the Fens have a long association with ice. Centuries ago, farmers unable to work the frozen land strapped flattened bones to their feet and punted themselves along dykes, waterways and ice-blasted marshes. During the nineteenth century bones were replaced with steel, screwed onto boots. It was the birth of the fen runner blades that would transform the sport.

The miracle of fen-skating is partly in the spontaneity of the occasion: the transformation of the countryside and the laws of nature that enable entire villages to walk on water. If the

opportunity is missed, it could be four or five years before conditions are right for skating again, until the people of the Fens
can, as Roger Deakin said, 'emerge like swallowtails or dragon-
flies, skimming about the frozen Fens with all the urgency of
Cinderella at the ball'.

Finally we reach a stretch where the water is green and ice-
free. We dip paddles silently. The sun is blindingly bright on the
river surface but gives off little heat. It creates a fantastic light-
show, though, the ripples from the water reflecting up onto the
bank. Pencil lines of gold slalom along with the reeds. The trees
on the bank are ice-rimed and although the banks are high, the
river again penned, nature has been allowed a foothold. Here
the floodplain has been given back to the Lark and it is full of
life. Rafts of ducks laugh away at speed and moorhens dash
from bank to bank with a *derka derka derka* splash, not quite
swimming, not quite flying. To our right rooks fill an old poplar
tree: giant black buds with wings folded tight.

Although the river is straight, almost canalised, it is beautiful. We stop paddling to watch two buzzards lope into the
air, circling with cattish mews. There are teal, kingfisher and
lapwing. Beneath it all is a dirge of industry, a didgeridoo hum
of tractors and pumps. This place has always been noisy with
the continual tump-tump-tumping of pumps lifting water from
fields to river.

The Fens have been drained for centuries; systems of dykes
and pumps were put in place in the 1600s to take away water

to prevent flooding and allow cultivation of the rich peat. The locals were furious, seeing the drainage as a direct threat to wildfowling, fishing and reed-cutting. A group called the Fen Tigers took matters into their own hands, tearing down sluices and filling ditches – even torching reed beds to prevent work taking place. But by the end of the seventeenth century much of the project had been completed. As the water drained away, the peat dried and contracted, the land slumping ever lower. Bigger pumps were brought in; wind was replaced by steam, diesel and electricity. The land continued to shrink – the Fens are now said to be the lowest point in Britain.

It's hard to imagine how this river would have looked before farming and drainage. In prehistoric times it would have been a delta, much like the Danube, a wild landscape of sluggish rivers, meres and reed swamp; a mass of braided channels fanning out over the land. Reminders still remain, if not in the river, then in the fields. Ribbons of grey silt called 'rhodons' can still be seen from the air, cutting across the arable expanse.

I've always felt that there is a strangeness in the Fens. The flatness is unreal, stretching out to the curve of the earth. The horizon pushed back and giant. It's the kind of place where you could watch your dog run away for a day.

The river is ruler-straight all the way to Prickwillow, a place name that fills James with tremendous joy. He titters from the front of the canoe every time it's mentioned. We arrive at about 3 p.m. The whole village seems battened down for winter.

No one is about; they're either hunched by fires or perhaps swallowtailing it up with skates on some frozen backwater. I had wanted to look around the drainage museum but a sign says it is closed until May, something that doesn't seem to disappoint James. But Prickwillow – its name coming from the prickets of willow that were harvested around here for thatch – is itself a museum, or a monument to this region's battle with water.

Before the nineteenth century the Great Ouse flowed here from Ely, rejoining the modern course of the river at Littleport. Then in 1829 the river was diverted and the old channel filled in and ploughed. The village today is built on this ghost of a river bank. The parish, like much of Fenland, lies below sea level, and it took pumping engines at the base of the newly dug drain linked to the Lark to keep the land dry. But there has been a price to pay. In the 1920s it was reported that the dry peat was sinking by two inches every year. At the village's vicarage it's clear to see how the land has peeled away from buildings like lips from teeth. Built originally without any steps, two were soon added to the front door, until a whole flight stretched from the shrinking earth. The land is now so low and the water table so high that the local dead can no longer be interred at Prickwillow's church. Burials instead take place on the Isle of Ely, its lofty height of 128 feet offering an eternal view of a collapsing landscape.

∽

From Prickwillow it is an easy paddle to the mouth of the Lark and within ten minutes we reach the junction with the Ouse. We drift onto it, under a bridge, causing the pigeons furtling about underneath to take to the air with wing beats like soft hand-claps. A swan, busy fluffing its wings on the bank, shimmies down to the water and launches itself ahead of us with a regal plop, its neck arched back and chest puffed out. The old expression about this bird's grace doesn't quite work close up. Although the churning, flat paddle feet are out of sight, he jerks along in haughty bursts like a clutch-heavy driver.

For the last few miles the Lark has been a good 60 feet across, but here on the Ouse – one of the four great rivers of England, along with the Severn, the Thames and the Trent – it is wider still. A character in Graham Swift's novel *Waterland* said that the river's name exudes slowness: 'A sound which invokes quiet flux, minimum tempo; cool, impassive, unmoved motion. A sound which will calm even the hot blood racing in your veins.'

'Ouse,' I say, 'Ooooooouse.'

James gives me a look.

We hang about in the middle of the channel taking it all in, looking at the sign that points left to Ely and right to Denver. The train tracks follow the river's course, the electricity that powers them held up by a corridor of supports like goal posts. It is easy to see why someone might say this landscape is bleak or uninteresting: the flat, featureless land and water roll endlessly on. But the sense of scale is powerful, perhaps even sublime. The sight of the river merging into the sky is both captivating and disturbing; an aesthetic of discomfort that comes from the knowledge that what you're seeing is unbalanced, both aesthetically and environmentally. We turn the canoe, watching the dancing ripples created by the paddles' bite, and head back upstream.

The temperature on the river is dropping quickly, the light shrinking away like the slumping land of the Fen. We're not going to make it back to the car, we're going to have to camp. The surroundings that seemed so hospitable, so full of light and life, are now tinged with menace. Ominous. I imagine an aerial view of the river and shudder. The thin band of green against endless flat fields of black earth. Frosted by a cold Fenland wind with nothing to stop it but our hunched backs. The land and the water are braced for night.

Nearly two miles south of Prickwillow we glide towards a bank and drag the canoe onto land. My hands, wet from beaching the Pipe, are already hurting from the cold. I huff on them, jam them under my armpits, stuff them into my trousers. But nothing works. My fingers are leaden. Clumsy. Trying to tie the hammock knots is nothing short of torture, the simple shoelace bow falling through frozen digits. We light the portable wood-burner that James has made from an old ammunition box, giving the sputtering survival matches a helping hand with a generous slug of meth from the stove. The flames shoot from the metal chimney, a fire flash that burns into our retinas and curls the hairs on the back of my hands. It's strange how a small fire can almost instantly transform a camp. The fire is a tiny red-hot flag of ownership. For now this patch of the dark, sinking Fens is ours alone. It is home.

Actually, I'm surprised how much I think of home on these trips. On the Stour, I remember feeling almost disappointed that I missed it. What kind of explorer wants to be both on the edge of the unknown and eating at his own table with his own family? I am, I thought wretchedly at the time, nought but a softy. But I'm not alone. Shortly after the Antarctic explorer Ernest Shackleton had left for his expedition in 1907, he wrote to his wife: 'My darling wife. Your dear brave face is before me now and I can see you just as you stand on the wharf and are smiling at me my heart was too full to speak and I felt that I wanted just come ashore and clasp you in my arms and love and care for you.'

I look at my own slightly pathetic text messages to Jen after just less than twelve hours away. 'Frrrrrreeeeeezing, miss you all. Love you xxxxxxx.'

Writing in *Desert and Ice*, Yi Fu Tuan suggests that the idea of home is vital for any exploration. It is the solid base for a point of departure; it provides a sense of security that might even drive a desire for the alien and the inhospitable. And camp, for all its failings – the leaks, the muck, the gathering ice – is a home away from home. It satisfies that need for familiarity and comfort in sharp contrast to whatever is outside the wooden or canvas walls. Looking at James as we shimmy round the stove, I know there are very few places I would rather be.

I check my phone. Jen has texted back: 'Kids being pain in backside.' Another message blinks through while I'm deciding how to reply. 'Stay warm. Try not to die xxx.'

The hammock is stiff with ice when I wake in the morning, the zip jammed by the haw on the outside and the moisture from my own frozen breath. I jiggle around, thrashing and swearing. Outside the world has been sugared. Everything is crisp and white. The tarpaulin crackles with ice. The freeze has sent ice shooting across the river, a paper-thin shelf running from the bank towards the middle of the flow. We drink tea and eat a cold breakfast while we pack, eager to head out onto the river.

We're nearly back at Isleham when we see the kingfisher. He perches in a clump of bramble as we glide slowly towards him. The colours are truly beautiful, like crushed shells and powdered lapis lazuli. A brighter streak of blue runs down his back, splashing like water drops over wings and head. His cheeks are blushed with the same burnt orange that paints his chest. Folk tales claim that the marks are the result of flying too close to the sun. He is almost too perfect to exist. I only found out recently that the feathers of the kingfisher aren't actually pigmented blue; their startling colour comes from the Tyndall effect – the process of light being scattered in a particular way by the feathers' particles. If it wasn't for this, the kingfisher would be what birders commonly refer to as a 'brown job'.

This time we follow the river's old course through the marina at Isleham to avoid the iced-up lock, navigating the sluice and disturbing fishermen by driving the loudest and most excitable geese I've ever met towards their dipped rods. The air is thick with coal smoke belching from the blackened stove pipes of moored boats. I love the grandness and romance of their names: 'The Emperor', 'Belladonna' . . . 'Wendy'. We hug the right bank as we follow the Lark's course back towards Jude's Ferry. Out of the corner of my eye I see something. It looks like a gravestone, perched by the side of the river next to a broken pump. Curious, we steer into the bank and I scramble onto land while James steadies the canoe. I push back the grass and wipe away flaking scales of lichen that fill and blur the carved words. I read out the inscription to James: 'The Rev Charles Haddon Spurgeon, The Prince of Preachers was baptised here, 3 May 1850.'

I feel pleased to have found the spot here in the Holy Land of the English, a physical reminder of when the river was the Jordan of the Fens. With its old monasteries, its churches and cathedrals, from Crowland to Ely, Peterborough, Ramsey and Thorney, God has loomed large over this flat land for centuries.

Before this trip I put it down simply to the need for hope: the golden rope that would pull Fenlanders from their sinking earth, from the slime and shit of eel baskets and the hellish din of the pumps to something better. But now I feel differently.

This river, widened, narrowed, sucked dry, polluted, ignored and forgotten, still stirs up spirituality. It still has power. It can still be resurrected. For all the despair I have felt on this journey at the Lark's treatment, there have also been reasons for hope: the signs of care; the hard work to heal and restore the river's flow, to make it sing again.

CHAPTER 4

Spirit of the river

I t is trying to rain as we turn off the main road and lope over a muddy track. A miserable, wind-blown drizzle. A mizzle. The path bends past a scrapyard filled with shipping containers and broken-down cars. To the right, the double lines of rail track race each other to the horizon. We cross and head over a stile and past an old wall, shoulder blades of dry stone jammed together and crusted with thick skins of bright white lichen. In front of us the field slopes up to a small copse with a straggling line of old thorns tracking through the centre. And then we see it. A stone, guarded by an old ash: a flecked marble plinth that marks the source of the Thames: 'The Conservation of the River Thames 1857–1974. This Stone Was Placed Here to Mark the Source of the River Thames.'

Directly in front of it is a small pit lined with stone. There are records that a well stood in Trewsbury Mead as late as the eighteenth century, surrounded by a wall measuring some

eight feet. The wall was demolished, eroded or shouldered
down by cattle, and the well filled in, leaving just this tiny
Andy Goldsworthy circle of oolite stone; a font to hold and
offer up clear water, a cairn signifying both beginning and
end.

River sources are places of intrigue, portals from the underworld to this world, where water pulses, pumps or just trickles
from mysterious beds to glint and dance in the sun. They are
places of transition from the dark to the light, the starting point
of a symbolic circle that sees a river rise to journey to the sea
and return with the rain. In Norse mythology 'Hvergelmir',
which means something like 'bubbling boiling spring', is the
origin – the source – of all living things and the place to which
everything will eventually return. But behind all the power
and personality there has also been wonder; a sense of human
curiosity at how something so great and powerful could spring
from something so small. After all, to journey to a source is to
go backward – against the flow.

I start mentally to rewind the Thames, imagining it as a
gigantic bore, tearing itself from the sea and slithering inland;
shedding Dartford's bridge, tunnels and tolls; barging aside
barriers and unravelling the histories of London, Kingston,
Walton, Staines, Windsor; wriggling free from the concrete
casing of towns that cling to its banks: Maidenhead, Marlow
and Henley; Reading, Wallingford, Abingdon; the dreaming
spires of Oxford. I watch it shrink from its widest point of

18 miles at Foulness Point to 60 feet at Lechlade, dwindling further as it closes in on Cricklade and Trewsbury Mead; past eighty islands; through forty-five locks and under 134 bridges, its history borne like black silt.

It will take about nineteen days for the river to journey to London from this field. I feel it wash over me, some 215 miles of water. Forty million years of history returning to where it all starts. Or does it? About 11 miles upstream, the permanent springs at Seven Springs, the welling-up point of the Churn – a tributary of the Thames – also boast a memorial stone, its more poetic inscription reading: *'Hic tuus o Tamesine pater septemgeminus fons'*; *'Here, O Father Thames, [is your] seven-fold source'.* This alternative source would make the Thames 229 miles to the Severn's 220. Traditionally, however, the source is considered to be here at Trewsbury Mead, which, as Peter Ackroyd writes in his book *Thames: Sacred River*, has 'from earliest times [. . .] been celebrated, or sanctified, because of its flowing waters'.

Today, though, the source is dry, the stones wet only from the rain. The infant Thames sleeps. The loss of woods and their condensing effects, together with abstraction, may have played a part in making the sight of water at the source less common, but heavy rain will still tempt the Thames from its bed. In photographs taken during the 1960s, small boys can be seen paddling canoes around the ash tree, while a postcard I bought at the Thames Head pub where we are staying shows pools, or at least impressive puddles, that were photographed in the winter of 2001.

We take pictures of each other standing by the marking stone and a wooden sign showing the 180-mile distance to the Thames Barrier. This is the final destination for those on the Thames Walk but for us it is just the beginning. Tomorrow we will dip paddles in liquid history and travel from the quiet meanders of Cricklade to the start of the navigable Thames at Lechlade; a small exploration of a river that has supported and nurtured humans since man and woman first tramped across the land bridge that connected England to mainland Europe. A place of worship and wonder, of beauty and art, trade and filth, freedom and conflict. A border on its north bank with Gloucestershire, Oxfordshire, Buckinghamshire, Middlesex and Essex; while to the south, the counties of Wiltshire, Berkshire, Surrey and Kent. A military boundary the Saxon British defended in vain against Caesar and also a spiritual boundary. A place that, judging by the barrows along its length, was believed to help the dead cross between worlds.

I expected this early stretch of the Thames to crawl and gurgle but today it is bloated and swollen, banging its fists in a colicky fury, pocked by brown whirlpools and quivering eddies. Branches toboggan downstream at speed, clunking through fallen trees and spinning off banks. I wonder if it's just the energy from the 'fleet-footed' Churn joining the Thames and if the water will be calmer away from Cricklade. But I already know the answer. This is a river in spate; we could be in for a rough ride.

We edge the Pipe in cautiously down the slipway, James dipping his paddle while I rudder from behind, leaning the canoe into the centre of the river. The banks are lined with a thin band of reeds, long blonde eyelashes that flutter in the breeze. Through them I can see where the river has surged over its banks to lap over crops and under trees, blurring the lines between land and water. River country.

Getting the Pipe to move in the right direction is proving difficult. With less gear and more water she is twitchy – too eager to please, fishtailing round corners as we paddle too fast for the current. A dog walker had warned us about fallen trees while we unloaded the car. Although we have navigated rivers more congested than this – both the Waveney and the Lark – here there is no time to stop and think, to read the river and choose careful routes. We depend on instinct. If we hesitate we get stuck, it seems, so instead we bulldoze through, willow branches and brambles whipping round our faces as we speed into narrow gaps – ducking our heads down and waiting, hoping, for the battery to stop. We emerge from each blockage travelling ever faster, with less time to negotiate the next bend or the next log; it is a vicious, churning cycle.

The calmness I've previously felt on entering a river, that sensation of slipping gradually into a different, gentler world, doesn't come here. There is no slow, suckering detachment from the mundane. No mellow thoughtfulness. Instead we are grabbed by the scruffs of our necks and hurled forward to be broken on bridges and tree limbs. The river is wild and dark.

The name Thames even hints at its murkiness, deriving from the Middle English 'Temese', which itself could spring perhaps from the Celtic 'Tamesas', meaning dark. The Tamar, Teme and Thame, a tributary of the Thames, probably all share the same root. The names of rivers are some of our oldest words: the Ouse comes from the Celtic word 'usso', for water, while the Avon simply means river.

The Pipe shoots from a bend onto a flat piece of water, a lake that I hadn't spotted on the map when I checked it this morning. The current bleeds away. A vapour trail of white bubbles that marked the route of the river's flow – like some kind of submerged monster swimming in front of us – has disappeared. James scans the horizon and turns to face me.

'Where do we go?'

I shrug in reply. We paddle on slowly, not wanting to venture too far in the wrong direction. It is relaxing, easy work after what has been an unexpectedly ferocious start. The first chance to really think about being on the river. Except we're not on the river. James realises what has happened before I do.

'Ah,' he says thoughtfully, 'I think you'd better look down.'

Without the brown whirl of the current, the water beneath the canoe is clear, and through it I can see line after neat line of old maize stems, occasionally breaking the surface like fibrous snorkels. We're paddling across a field. The river has shrugged us off, sending us skidding through a hole in the bank and onto a farmer's field without us even noticing. To the left, about 100 yards away, a line of crack willows look like they could mark the route of the river and we paddle over. Beneath us, over a lip of grass, is the river, its surge contrasting with the calmness of the water we're currently paddling.

We stick to our route, looking for an opening where we might be able to slip back onto the Thames. This field must have been underwater for some time. The topsoil looks as if it has completely gone: another reminder of how quickly water can re-wild. We find a hole in the bank, the water tumbling out of the river onto the land; the power of its flow cutting a step into the field. We push hard against it, forcing our way back into the river, feeling the resistance give way to the downstream current that picks us up again with watery hands and passes us on and on.

The drizzle of yesterday has lifted and the sky is pale blue, clouds hanging like wool on wire, teased and combed by the breeze but hardly moving. A red kite turns above us, or rather its tail does. Pulled as if by strings, it dips a trembling fishtail and wheels over the river, flashing its rich red chest and milky-white throat. Despite the blockages we're making good time.

The trip across the field has taken us past fallen trees and a wriggling bend that in these conditions could have been tricky. It feels like we're getting used to the river too. We gain in confidence, leaning into bends and paddling out of them. The water surges up round the Pipe's nose to fan and lap out behind us like a wet brown skirt.

At Castle Easton, the church of St Mary the Virgin is nearly dipping its toe in the water, its stone gold blushed with pink. A site of Christian worship since the twelfth century, it is a place that was probably special for people long before that.

Rivers have often been connected with the spiritual world, sources of life and of death. It's one of the reasons there are so many gods, nymphs and myths associated with them. According to legend, for example, the Wye, the Severn and the River Ystwyth all share the same story: all three were nymphs conceived from mist, rain, snowmelt, moss and marsh and born to the Lord of the Mountains, Plynlimon. When the day came for them to leave their home, to set out into the world, Ystwyth headed west, taking the shortest route to the coast, meeting the Irish Sea by the town that would take her name. Hafren went next, winding through England and Wales, travelling for long miles until she reached the Bristol Channel; her shimmering route became known as the Severn. But the third daughter,

Vaga (the Latin name of Wye and meaning wandering), wanted neither to rush nor spend time in the world of men. Instead she chose a quieter route, whispering through hills and crags, seeking out the wild places where beauty lived on. She sang through valleys and forests: a song for the porpoising otter; for the salmon; for the curtseying bob of the dipper; and for the kingfisher, whose jewelled back she softly kissed. She danced and darted, joyful, serene, all the way to Hafren, who rushed back upstream to meet her and guide her on, towards the sea.

History overflows with rivers that are regarded as either being divinities or possessing other-worldly powers. It should be no surprise that the Thames had the same treatment. No one is quite sure when Old Father Thames was first evoked, but there is plenty to suggest that those living by the river have been paying their dues for hundreds if not thousands of years. An Iron Age shield was dredged from the depths at Battersea in 1857 and ancient votive offerings are still constantly being uncovered along the river, picked from the strandline by mud-larks and archaeologists.

Perhaps its personification as a god, or the creation of myths around it, was a way of understanding the river and its changes; the act of worship an attempt to control or impose order on water that has the power to shape and fertilise land, to give life and to take it away. The divine river helped make sense of the mystery, the beauty and the destruction of the natural world.

Some suggest that Old Father Thames has links to other gods. Peter Ackroyd says Father Thames 'bears a striking resemblance to the tutelary gods of the Nile and the Tiber'. The Roman river god Tiberinus certainly shares key characteristics with him: the beard, the locks, the aversion to clothes. Ackroyd suggests that Old Father Thames's hipsterish follicles could represent the braiding channels of the river's flow. But whatever his past, Old Father Thames has come to be a personification of the river in both good times and bad. He has been seen as a revered guardian while also caricatured as a rude and filthy tramp, during the pollution of the nineteenth century, surrounded by dead fish and rotting livestock, offering up his children Diphtheria, Cholera and Scrofula to those who lived and worked on his waters.

We continue on slowly, taking a left bend, with the sun gilding water that is retreating from the fields. The current, no longer funnelled by obstacles, slows to a glugging jog. At Kempsford there is another church named for St Mary, where Edward I, Edward II, Henry IV and Chaucer were all said to have worshipped.

The arrival of Christianity may have meant the disavowal of the old gods, but the rivers continued to be sacred places, with plenty of churches built on their banks. The Thames is certainly a river of saints. A swelter of them. Birinus, apostle to the Saxons of the west, who baptised converts at Kemble and Somerford Keynes; St Alban, Britain's first Christian martyr, who parted the waters on the way to his execution; St Frithuswith, Frideswide, Frideswith, Fritheswithe, Frevisse, or just Fris, founder of Oxford Priory and patron saint of Oxford University, who summoned a holy spring from the earth. Relics too have found their way to the water's edge, from the spear tip that was said to have punctured the side of Christ, to the skeletal hand of James the Apostle. But on this stretch, it seems that St Mary holds sway. The Mother of God on the mother of rivers.

There is a dark side to the river's spiritual connection – stories that hint not only at its role as a link between worlds but also its propensity to take life, a waterscape of ghosts and untimely death. In the thirteenth century Henry Plantagenet, Earl of Lancaster, was said to have stabbed his wife Maud to death and thrown her body in the Thames after believing (in error) that she had taken a lover. Then, in the fourteenth century, the son of Henry's son, Henry – also confusingly called Henry – drowned here. Consumed by grief, his father (the second Henry) decided to leave the painful memories behind and rode to join the war with France. As he left Kempsford his horse lost a shoe, which the villagers picked up and nailed to the church door, where it still remains. The sister of the drowned boy, also called Maud, is said to haunt this river too, floating along Lady Maud's Walk on moonlit nights, waiting for her sibling to return. Other stories suggest that the spectre is Henry's murdered wife (the first Maud), who lives on as the Lady of the Mist.

Rivers, where the boundaries of life and death are worn thin to transparency, attract such stories. In Norfolk there is the ghost of a thief who drowned while escaping, his body weighed down with stolen jewels. In Gwent the spectre of a homeless man who fell into the river is said to repeatedly walk his final route. On the Thames, at the site of the Old London Bridge, it is claimed that the cries and screams from a thirteenth-century sinking can still be heard. Not far away at Traitors' Gate – a place where high-ranking prisoners once left the water and entered the Tower of London – there have been modern sightings of people in Tudor clothes, guarded by spear-wielding soldiers. There are countless other ghosts linked to battles, broken hearts and suicides; reports of disembodied voices, strange mists and hovering lights. I wonder if these stories are rooted in our belief that the river is a Stygian flow, a boundary between earth and the underworld. Or perhaps it is just because bad things happen on the water. The spirits, or the tales of them, are a memory – and a warning.

Downstream the height of the water almost makes the stone bridge impassable: the river effectively lowers its triple arches and creates barricades of woven branches. None shall pass. It takes three attempts to get through, the Pipe pitching and wobbling nervously as we lie back, our faces inches away from dripping bricks.

The Thames is a river of bridges. In total, there are 134 from source to sea, funnelling the water round their piers to create glassy eddies and hypnotic swirls. Bridges have always been incredibly important structures, not just as crossing points but as symbolic markers, reinforcing a river's spiritual and religious importance. They seem to have been places where people thought that the rivers and their gods needed appeasing. All sorts of offerings, including swords, scabbards and figurines, have been pulled from beneath London's bridges. Chapels were also built on them, perhaps in recognition of the continuing sacredness of the water. There is still something of the old ways about bridges; they still have the power to attract people and their votive offerings. And it is to bridges that the desperate are also drawn to offer up their own lives, a final tragic step into and away from darkness.

We speed towards more downed trees, their branches raking the water as the river bends and twists like a pinned snake. I aim for a narrow gap under a tree, its arched branch the colour of oxidised copper. It looks like a clear route through. James ducks under and then shoots out a hand, trying to slow our pace – there's another fork of wood we hadn't seen spearing from the water. The blockage is what canoeists call a strainer: while the hole is big enough to let water through, it is too small for a canoe. It all happens in the blink of an eye but it feels like minutes. The nose of the Pipe hits the sunken branch and twists, the back end swinging round, horizontal to the flow. The current rushes in – seizing its chance – throwing itself against the side and at the same time pushing up under the leaning, lowered edge. I watch James fall with a shout and feel the canoe going from under me. I start to stand, reaching towards the side that is already rising out of the water, ready to roll. It's too late. We're in.

The water fills my vision. Brown, rushing and cold. It squeezes my chest, forcing out the air in a croaked holler. I cough and splutter, clearing water out of my nose and lungs, gasping again, and then hitting out with frantic hands as floating branches nudge into me like curious fish. I look for James. He has surfaced about ten feet away. I can see the shock in his eyes; can hear the same ragged breaths as he treads water. The river has already taken both us and the Pipe – upside down but afloat – past the fallen tree and is now whirling us downstream.

I shout above the noise of the flow.

'You alright?'

'Yeah . . . But we've got to get her back over.'

Desperately we try again and again to right her, straining under her gunnels and kicking for all we're worth. On the fourth or fifth time the Pipe starts to turn, but the roll is too slow and too low. She pitches and wallows, water rushing in to fill her up. She's going down and there's nothing we can do. We take deep breaths and force ourselves under the water, pushing our knees under the Pipe's bottom to try and lever her back to the surface. It takes almost everything we've got but we're desperate not to let her go. Our breathing is noisy. Shocked, rasping, frightening. Only our heads are above the surface as we drift along cradling the sunken canoe. I can't help but think that we've already been in the water too long, that our body heat is leaching away. It is cold, dangerously so. We have to sort this. We have to get out.

We make another attempt to swim to the side, both of us kicking hard, but the current is too strong, we just can't shake its grip. It pulls us further and further downstream in a conveyor belt of twigs and brown water. As the river widens we're swung to the outside of a bend. I can see where the water, the current churning and sucking, has cut away the bank to form a muddy cave, topped with a fragile grass shelf. A willow, undermined and toppled, lies with its branches across the river. We stick to it like flies on a windscreen, half-clambering, half-swimming for a limb strong enough to hold us. With my back to the flow I can feel more debris coming down the river, weaving me into the blockage, while bouncing off the canoe. We have been reduced to flotsam.

Although we're just yards from the bank I can't see how we can get out without letting go of the canoe. James is panting hard. His head is lowered over the sunken canoe.

'I just can't do anything,' he shouts, almost to himself. I test another branch, groaning as the rotten wood gives way beneath my hand and is whisked away by the water. The noise is tremendous, battering and numbing me as much as the cold.

'What the fuck are we going to do?'

I wonder if we should let go, to see if the river will carry us somewhere where it's easier to get to the bank. But we've already been swept some 200 yards downstream. We're exhausted. I can feel my breathing is getting laboured. My whole body is shuddering, shaking from the core as it tries to regulate its heat. I know it's a good sign, but how long will it last? How long before hypothermia starts to kick in, dulling our minds and our bodies? I can hear James kicking about in the water and he manages to find a sunken foothold, an underwater branch. He drags himself half out of the river, his clothes sagging, and makes his way along the toppled willow. He heaves the Pipe, trying desperately to get her nose up. But the weight of the water inside her is making it almost impossible. I try and help, pushing with my shoulders and hands, but I have nothing to brace myself against and I can feel my feet rising to the surface with every desperate, pathetic effort. I grab a bag and a paddle and hold onto the tree, almost just waiting to see what will happen.

Then the barking comes, at first distant and then loud and constant. I can see him now. A furry, wiry muzzle and eyes like black coal. He's a big, rangy, lolloping fuzzy-wig of a dog. I can hear his owners shouting at it; to come; to shut up. But his din is more than welcome and we holler back. James has now managed to get completely out of the river, but he's having to pull the canoe over the tree and onto the bank by himself. Its bulk is blocking my only way out of the water. My mind feels fogged, waterlogged. I know I need to get out but I've almost stopped caring, the urgency has gone from my body. I can feel the siren song of the river, the ancient nymphs and sprites pulling at my arms and legs, tugging, urging me home.

I can see people running along the bank. Past the dog, still barking. A gun dog signalling downed, flapping birds to his master. A man joins James and grabs hold of the end of the canoe, pulling it up enough so I can get closer to the bank. I throw the paddle and bag and James grabs me by both wrists as my feet scramble and kick over a mud-spattered tree trunk. But there's no relief at being out of the water. My clothes are shrink-wrapped round me. Every time I move I can feel the cold bleeding into my bones. I know I need to get out of them, but the idea of undressing or taking anything off fills me with dread. Instead I bend over, arms wrapped round myself. I can hear James talking to me, or the family that are helping us, but I can't think of anything apart from the cold. It's different from the Alde and the Lark when the frost pinched and bit. I just feel drunk on it. Like my veins have been sucked dry.

The man must have introduced himself because suddenly we're calling him Rob. He helps drag the Pipe up onto the bank and turn it over. Our dry clothes have gone, along with a paddle, while the bags holding our phones are full to the brim. The screens are dead. I try to think about where we are, the distance to the road, how long it will take us to get warm clothes, to plan something; but part of me just wants to curl up on the river bank and go to sleep.

Rob sends his family off to continue their walk and helps us carry the Pipe back to his house, where he says we can warm up and call a taxi. We haul the canoe for a mile over fields, levering it over fences, Rob stepping in when James or I start to flag, sweating and shivering at the same time.

Rob has only lived by the river for about a year and has only canoed it in summer. Today has given him second thoughts about trying in winter or with his young son. He has, he says, a new respect for what the river can do. I imagine he thinks we are experienced hands rather than foolhardy novices. He leads us into a utility room and hands us towels, telling us not to worry when we apologise again for ruining his walk and dripping on his floor. He switches on a blow heater and leaves to call a cab to take us into town.

Once we have arrived at a hotel in Lechlade we turn the heating on full and drape our clothes over every radiator. We have bought bags of rice from a garage shop and pour it into a pair of old tights left behind by a previous guest, tucking our damp phones inside and suspending them from the radiator like a pair of gigantic bollocks. No matter what we do, we just can't warm up; the heat leaks from our cores like power from a dodgy battery. We head to the bar to call Jen and James's girl-friend Anna and then sit by the fire in silence, nursing drinks and feeling sorry for ourselves. The relief of simply being alive has already given way to frustration and embarrassment, both at being caught out and for losing so much gear.

I walk outside to watch the river. It's getting dark but I can still see the rush and the pull of the water. The swirl and lick. A constant, almost hypnotising flow, sweeping under the bridge and towards the lock that marks the beginning of the navigable Thames. I wonder if my paddle will make it this far, returning to me like Thor's hammer.

Whether it is our lucky escape or thinking about ghosts earlier in the day, I can't help but think about how many bodies the Thames has borne away. It's a gloomy secret only the river knows. Over the years almost every conceivable body part has been dredged from its waters. A nose. A forearm. A pelvis. A chin. Every week at least one body is found somewhere along the Thames, pulled from the water or deposited on its banks, evidence of an accident, murder or suicide – perhaps the call of the river's spirits was just too much. I shiver – my coat is still steaming on a radiator – and head back to the fire.

The next morning we strike out for St John's Lock to complete the journey. We walk almost in silence, the river still surging and jostling its banks. James didn't sleep well: the realisation of how dangerous and unprepared we were sank in. This all feels a world away from Stevenson and Simpson and the haughty jollity of *Three Men in a Boat*. For the first time, our little adventures seem a bit much. There's an unspoken fear that we have bitten off more than we can chew; our bravado has been washed away. But I know it's an important experience too. It feels as if we have discovered something meaningful: that the Thames is not what we thought. That beneath the history, the centuries of stories and tales that have hardened like a crust on lava, making it a solid, single, sensible thing, primal nature still flows. We may have lost some gear and our confidence, but we found the wild. We fell through the reflection and into the river.

Old Father Thames is looking rather casual when we find him; reclining back on his elbow, one knee tucked under his body. A sheet exposes a hint of stony pubis while he stares out moodily over the river. This statue, first commissioned for the grounds of the Crystal Palace in 1854, was moved to the source at Thames Head before being relocated here in the 1970s.

He now sits at St John's Lock as a monument, signifying a long and sometimes fraught relationship with a river that has flowed for millions of years and will no doubt do so long after the last human draws breath. I look at him again; at the metal spade resting on his shoulder – representing the digging of locks to make navigation possible, and at his glowering, fox-terrier face.

'Well here he is,' I say, leaning forward to touch his knee.

It feels like we should make an offering for future safe passage, but he has already snatched away a paddle and a bag of kit. James is in a less conciliatory mood.

'You old bastard, we'll be back for you.'

CHAPTER 5

A world transformed

The Thames is a river transformed. No longer the wild, rain-swollen rush of Cricklade but a dark, even flow that reflects grey, wind-frayed clouds and hisses away under the canoe. We have been transformed too. It is two weeks since we nearly joined the ghosts of the Thames and our kit has been overhauled: jeans swapped for drysuits; floats purchased and fitted to the Pipe and our beloved carrier bags replaced with roll-top dry bags. Last weekend we spent a cold Sunday purposefully overturning the Pipe in the Stour before throwing it back over and climbing in, leaping, kicking and wriggling into the rocking canoe. I feel slightly apprehensive, or at least cautious, being back on the water. My body seems stiffer than it should be; the paddle strokes are snatched and out of time with James's. But the river is calm. Easy.

I'm always amazed at how easily the riverscapes can be transformed: from terrifying torrents to gentle flows; from summery idylls to icy death traps; and from polluted waste-lands to bustling wildlife thoroughfares. The story of rivers is one of continuous transformation.

To our left is the low wooden building of the Royal Canoe Club at Teddington where I spent two or three hours this morning going through their archives. It is the oldest canoe club in the world and one of its founder members was John MacGregor, whose 1866 book, *A Thousand Miles in the Rob Roy Canoe*, effectively brought about the birth of modern canoeing and kayaking. The club still has his original notebooks and it was these I went to see: pages full of a scratchy, spiky hand in black ink that describes the waters of the Nile and the Danube. There were illustrations too, beautiful pastel-coloured drawings of craggy rocks and spindly pines, rolling waves or a musta-chioed man tackling cascades with a stiff upper lip and a straw boater.

The driving ambition of his book, 'to describe a new mode of travelling ... by which new people and things are met with, while healthy exercise is enjoyed', is still deeply relevant. MacGregor's description of a 'strange feeling of *freedom*' when pushing off into the tide at Gravesend at the start of the tour is one that strikes a chord with me some 150 years later: a sense of liberation, of not being bounded by sea 'shallow and shore'. It was MacGregor's writing that directly inspired Robert Louis Stevenson's trip across Belgium and France. From the Rob Roy to the Arethusa and the Cigarette, there has been a trickle-down of inspiration that whetted Deakin's and my own appetite for travelling on water.

From the canoe club it doesn't take long to reach Teddington Lock and the start of the lower Thames, the point of the river's transformation from inland flow to tidal rush. This lock gate was once fiercely guarded. The first keeper here was said to have been armed with a blunderbuss and a bayonet, the only means by which to extract a toll from surly fishermen and boatmen. Now, though, as we pull the Pipe up a small, rollered slipway and back down the other side towards the brown lower reaches of the Thames, the only sentry is the remains of a gull.

I guess I expected some big change in the water, but with the tide slack and soon to turn the river feels little different. Wider perhaps, sprawling around 300 feet to the embankments, but there are no raging currents, no surge in river traffic, just gentle brown water that glugs and glollops under the bottom of the canoe.

Yet if the water remains the same, the amount of wildlife already seems to have increased. Ducks throng around the canoe. Mallard drakes squabble and scoot after females, brutish brawlers who nip the necks of the hens with abusive passion. Mandarins, looking like an explosion in a make-up factory, zip away from the mêlée. Their faces are a riot of grease-paint reds, whites and green. They are lovers, not fighters, dressed to impress with burnt-orange tailcoats that flick away from their rumps in the manner of a Vivienne Westwood bustle.

Screaming parties of luminous green rose-collared parakeets fly across the river, trailing pronged tails like gigantic mayfly nymphs. They make the unholy racket of shrill, deflating balloons, with a hint of a Sooty and Sweep squeak. The whole experience is of a mish-mash. A glorious melting pot of wildlife: a first taste of cosmopolitan London.

At Twickenham we come to the first big island in the Thames: an ait or eyot. This is Eel Pie Island, a place where people of all kinds, of all standings, once congregated in summer to consume eels.

Many of the UK's rivers have strong associations with eels. The Fenlanders on the Lark and the Great Ouse depended on them, fishing with baited wicker traps that changed little for thousands of years. It is claimed that the name of Ely, the capital of the Fens – which we saw on the Lark, towering over the wetlands on its island of clay – has its roots in the Old Northumbrian word 'ēlġē', meaning 'district of eels'. But it is the Thames and the city it created that are now more closely tied to eels, the slime-covered cords that connected Londoners to the river.

Jellied eels are still as London as Buckingham Palace, Bow Bells and Big Ben, but eels are now a rarity in the Thames; the fish that are eaten now come from the flatlands of Holland or from Northern Ireland. The Zoological Society of London, which monitors populations by trapping and recording, suggests that eel populations in this river have declined by up to 95 per cent over the last twenty-five to thirty-five years. The species, whose young once thickened the dark waters of the Thames as they migrated from the Sargasso Sea, is classified as Critically Endangered by the International Union for Conservation of Nature Red List of Threatened Species; a victim of climate change, disease and man-made structures.

Downstream we slide alongside another eyot, the river's silky skin wrinkling under the canoe. Two trees have fallen to create natural groynes, their branches raking the water to collect black silt that has formed a steep beach and a sheltered bay. We manoeuvre the Pipe in closer, the wash sucking and slapping onto the bank, and get out to explore.

The eyot looks ideal: densely packed with trees and scrub. A hideout. A refuge. A place to camp. The ground, perhaps recently underwater, is soft, and the tide has deposited bottles and cans in a muddy wrack line that extends some 30 feet from the bank. The island smells of bark, dead leaves and cold; winter is still thawing in the middle of the Thames. Further in, through thorn and fallen branches, the island is firmer and tufted in soot-black moss, soft as fur. Poplars circle us, ivy tangling up straight trunks to brush leafless crowns. We pace between them, testing branches before deciding to string the hammocks up close together in front of an old ash. It's a striking tree. Shaped like a stag's head, bark hangs from its pronged branches like rags of half-shed velvet. There are treecreepers and bands of invasive parakeets, readying for roost.

The light had been fading on the river but the island is a place of perpetual gloom, the trees taking on the darkness of the Thames. We talk in low voices, settling into the surroundings, listening to the eyot's sounds and becoming familiar with its movements, getting to know the lie of the land. The island is small but it is often hard to see the river through the trees. We are truly hidden. Removed from both land and water.

On the island there is a feeling of delicious, harmless naughtiness. These kind of spaces seem designed for pirates and parrots, schemers and plotters. We are the highwaymen of the high waters, intentionally marooned. I wonder when the last person stepped onto this island. Days ago? Maybe weeks? Perhaps it hasn't been regularly visited since the great Frost Fairs between 1607 and 1814, when the Little Ice Age saw Old Father Thames freeze in his bed and whole towns assembled to skate and visit hastily erected shops and pubs. Ice many feet thick allowed Londoners to stride for miles across a riverscape transformed.

The biggest freeze came in the great winter between 1683 and 1684, when even the seas slushed with ice and froze solid for up to two miles from the shoreline. As in the Fens, the people of the Thames took to the river. The writer and diarist John Evelyn described how the ice was a scene of 'bull-baiting,

horse and coach races, puppet plays and interludes', rife with
'lewd places, so that it seemed a bacchanalian triumph or car-
nival on the water'. He writes too of the ice's impact on the
land, how it was a 'severe judgement' on the earth; the frozen
sap of trees caused trunks to explode, splitting timber as 'if
lightning-struck'.

It has been over a century since the last big Frost Fair. The
warming climate and the removal of the medieval London
Bridge – whose closely spaced piers collected ice and helped
dam the river's tidal flow – brought an end to the big freezes.
The last one of note was held for five days in 1814, when people
danced reels to the sound of fiddles, while others gathered in
drinking tents or sat by fires on the ice, warmed with rum and
grog.

We return to camp; the buzz of life from the banks slips
through the trees. Police sirens, a few shouts from early drinkers and the clumping whomp of swans coming into land. The
shriek of the parakeets is gradually replaced by the soft tip-tap
of rain on the tarps above us and the husky bark of a fox roam-
ing the south bank. I imagine him, his nails clip-clipping along
the Thames path, sniffing and rooting round bins, drinking in
the scents of the human world that he has made his own. I snap
on my torch to look for him, the red beam wobbling over the
water to the bank. Empty. I turn it off.

Although the light in the eyot dims, darkness never really
arrives at our camp. The glow from central London, still miles

downstream, colours the sky orange like a sun that never quite sets; like a phosphorescent foxfire – the spooky light of fungi in decaying wood. It is the shimmering orange ghost of burning ancient forests and long-dead sea creatures.

I wake early. There's now no need for trees to screen us. The fog, as much a part of London as any edifice of iron or stone, has rolled in and the world around us is completely changed once more. A pea-souper. It walls off the river from sight, a feathery grey barricade that limits our world to this circle of trees. The great stag tree is a mist-soaked wraith, a totemic shadow whose branches occasionally pierce the ground-scraping cloud as the wind moves off the river to creep and shiver through the wood. We realised last night that the island is on a flight path, with a plane passing over almost every minute. But now the fog dampens the sound of their approach until they fall out of the clouds almost on top of us, engines revving and screaming in preparation for landing, ribbons of cloud clinging to fuselage like wet rags.

James looks exhausted. He didn't sleep well, waking in the early hours with a fear that someone else was on the island: an eldritch feeling of being watched, a sense that our refuge had become a trap, each movement of the willows and the poplars transformed into murderous whispers. The ghosts of the river rising to the surface once more.

We are back on the river by half seven, paddling through the slowly lifting fog. A string of houses and a pub on the north bank, hidden by the island, emerge from the murk. A bare tree on the north bank contains a cluster of nests, a shanty town of sticks that look almost as if they have been swept there by an unfeasibly high tide. Perched in the branches are three cormorants. Two hold their wings out stiffly to dry, forming a crooked cross of black feathers. They don't seem bothered by the Pipe, allowing us to get close and glimpse the white markings that are the telltale sign of the breeding season. They look as if they have been leaning against a freshly painted wall.

There is something reptilian about cormorants, a knowing ancientness that unnerves the holy. In *Paradise Lost* Milton used the cormorant to symbolise Satan atop the Tree of Life, his first intrusion into Eden: 'Thence up he flew, and on the Tree of Life, / The middle Tree and highest there that grew, / Sat like a Cormorant; yet not true Life / Thereby regaind, but sat devising Death'. It was an association the cormorant, sometimes branded a 'doom bird', has struggled to shake off. Fishermen have persecuted it, blaming the bird for feasting on fish in aquatic farms and reservoirs, and lobbying for culls. Internet forums, always places of measured, level-headed reasoning, demanded that the 'black death' was shot and its roosts burnt. But as the UK is home to 13 per cent of the world's cormorant population – 41,000 wintering birds and 9,018 breeding pairs – calls for a general shooting licence have so far been resisted.

One of the birds lets out a bubbling, guttural bray and shifts its position on the branch. Perhaps you do have to look harder for the cormorant's beauty; to wait for the sun to expose the hint of colours hidden in its blackness. Cormorants aren't showmen either. Unlike the daring, breathtaking high dives of its relative, the gannet, the cormorant prefers to paddle rather than plunge, heading for the river bed with a craw filled with gravelly ballast. It is what the poet Amy Clampitt described as a 'bony pot-bellied arrow'. The roost tree is painted white with guano, a fishy, sticky, Copydex rime that makes the birds' blackness all the more stark. One turns its head, flashing a long beak that curves into a fish-hook barb, its eye sunscald bright.

At Putney I can feel James's rhythm at the front of the Pipe quickening. The swell around the bridge is higher than down-stream, but it doesn't feel like there's any need for urgency. I fall in with him regardless, my brain naturally following the new beat. He's still speeding up, his paddle a metronome, clicking against the pine gunwales and driving us forward with great scoops of water. We're going bloody fast. The water is slapping against the Pipe and her nose is now bouncing up and down, as if she is panting and tossing her head with effort. A fat, lazy horse kicked into a reluctant gallop.

Then I see what James is doing. Some 20 yards in front of us and to the left near the north bank is a rowing boat. A crew of ten young women are moving slowly in the water, their strokes long and languid, getting ready to stop and turn back upstream. But after watching boat after boat surge past at speed, their occupants oofing with effort and ignoring our cheery waves, James is taking this as an opportunity to exact revenge. We pull level with them and James, his arms whirring, locks eyes with the cox, his gritted-teeth grinning a silent challenge. A few of the girls watch us, smiling and sipping water as we bounce past, listening with one ear to the instructions drifting down from the cox. We are barely a length in front when I hear their oars clanking into position. Within three strokes they are past us, leaving the Pipe wobbling sadly in their wake. We might as well be in a bathtub. We begin to slow down, laughing, breathing hard.

'Thought we had them there for a minute,' James says, panting. 'Next time.'

The river is full of rowing boats today. In a few weeks' time the Boat Race, which has been held on the river between Putney and Mortlake since 1829, will take place and crews, coxes and commentators will check off timings against the bridges of Hammersmith and Barnes. The wind has risen and we are finding the going tough but, low in the water, the racing crews knife along regardless. We stick gamely to the right-hand side, pulling in, scraping banks to keep out of their way.

Approaching Fulham we see a single rower heading for us. He is on the wrong side of the river but we try to move for him, shouting for him to slow down and look behind. There is a rowing club right next to us and I'm sure he'll check for boats entering and leaving the water. He keeps coming.

'Watch out! Canoe behind! Canoe behind!'

His paddle catches the side of the Pipe and he explodes in fury.

'Why didn't you shout?' he demands.

'We bloody did,' we shout back, both of us slightly taken aback by his anger and attitude when it's us he ploughed into. His face, the colour and shape of boiled ham, reddens further. He wipes away a sweaty strand of greying hair and jabs an accusing finger at us.

'You said bugger all! Fucking morons,' he bellows, pulling on his oars again, his lycra top stretching to transparency over a belly considerably less streamlined than his boat. He is the kind of man who would hit his servants with a riding crop. Privileged, piggish; a right knob.

'What?' I shout back incredulous. 'Maybe have a look next time you're on the wrong side of a river and going past a club?'

He pulls another face at us, mocking and imitating our voices, before swearing at us again, his bravery and rudeness increasing incrementally with the distance he puts between himself and the Pipe. A man on the bank, getting ready to launch his own rowing boat, is doing his best to smother a laugh.

'Oh, didn't you know?' he says, affecting a mock bow. 'He owns this river.'

The exploded spire of the Shard appears and then disappears on the horizon like the beckoning finger of the capital. But it's the smokeless chimneys of Battersea Power Station on the south bank that give the first real sense of being in London proper. The cityscape transforming the experience of the river.

The banks here, for centuries a place of industry and trade, are still busy. But the nature of the work has changed. Almost every building has its own crane that stands like a giant tottering bird, constructing its nest girder by girder. Old crouches next to new. Sooty red brick against glass. The power station itself, one of the largest brick buildings in the world, is a spectacular monument to the filth and dirt of coal-fired power and old industry, but also a symbol of transformation on and of the Thames.

Many things have been planned for this iconic leviathan: a theme park; housing; shops; there were even rumours that Chelsea Football Club would build a new stadium here, with towering funnels capable of rivalling Wembley's old twin towers and its new 440-foot-high arch. But the building is now the centrepiece of a mile-long development of offices, hotels and apartment towers, a £9-billion project (more than the cost of staging the 2012 London Olympics) stretching from Vauxhall to Chelsea Bridge and served by its own Tube station. About a hundred people, including a few celebrities, have already moved in to part of the complex, named, for no obvious reason, Circus West Village. The power station building won't be open until 2020 – a place for leisure and shopping for the well-heeled and the curious. A glass elevator will take them to a viewing platform atop the chimneys.

The industry and ships that once created a forest of masts, a place where one could almost walk across the river from deck to deck, have long gone, scuppered and broken up by the wind-less creep of time. The river may still be at the heart of London's future here – many of the buildings are sail-shaped, formed of waves of glass that reflect back the dark waters of the Thames – but it is an exclusive future. The river views (at least on land) are owned by only the very wealthy.

Of course, it's not just the banks that have been trans-formed. The river is different too. The Thames remains dark but no longer is it filthy; no longer is it black and dead. For centuries the Thames accepted more than just ritualised offerings. Since at least Roman times human waste was piped into the river. As the population grew, so did the amount of effluent. London Bridge famously had long-drops built upon its length, and evi-dence of latrines has been found on many of its tributaries. The problems and the sickening smells of sludgy raw sewage, combined with waste from tanneries and butcheries, are well documented. But by the nineteenth century the situation had worsened. Modern industry, such as gas manufactories, had continued the habits of old, dumping by-products including cyanide and carbolic acid directly into the Thames. London may have been the biggest city in the world but the treatment of its waste had changed little since its founding. The effluent from three million people ran with the tide, washing upstream as far as Teddington, where revolting puddings of shit, up to six inches deep, lined the banks.

In a letter to *The Times* in 1855, written after travelling by steamboat from London and Hungerford Bridge, the scientist Michael Faraday said the 'appearance and smell' of the Thames had 'forced themselves at once on my attention'. Faraday, who described how 'the feculence rolled up in clouds' at St Paul's Wharf, Blackfriars Bridge, Temple Wharf, Southwark Bridge and Hungerford, conducted experiments with cards to test visibility in the river, with each white marker disappearing from sight just an inch from the surface.

'If there be sufficient authority to remove a putrescent pond from the neighbourhood of a few simple dwellings,' he wrote, 'surely the river which flows for so many miles through London ought not to be allowed to become a fermenting sewer . . . If we neglect this subject, we cannot expect to do so with impunity; nor ought we to be surprised if, ere many years are over, a season give us sad proof of the folly of our carelessness.'

Faraday's warning was ignored. In the end it took a heatwave, which caused the sewage of the Thames to cook and ferment, to put the problems of the river under the noses of the legislature. The stench was said to be unbearable. The *Journal of Public Health and Sanitary Review* reported 'strange stories flying of men struck down with the stench, and of all kinds of fatal diseases, upspringing on the river's banks'. At Westminster the smell became so bad that the curtains of Parliament were doused with a mixture of chloride and lime. A columnist for *The Times* reported how 'the intense heat had driven our legislators from the portions of their buildings that overlook the river. A few members, indeed, bent upon investigating the matter to its very depth, ventured into the library, but they were instantaneously driven to retreat, each man with a handkerchief to his nose.'

Chancellor Benjamin Disraeli himself was heard to complain about the 'Stygian Pool' of 'unbearable horror', while it was claimed that Queen Victoria was forced to abandon a pleasure cruise within minutes after falling foul of the great eggy stink of hydrogen sulphide guffing out of the oxygen-starved water. Although some thought was given to the idea of moving Parliament from its newly built home on the Thames to a more fragrant, less fluvial location, in the end common sense prevailed. A bill was signed that would see the reformation of the Thames through the design of a new sewage system – by the engineer Sir Joseph Bazalgette – and the construction of London's embankments, opened in 1865 by the soon-to-be commodore of the Royal Canoe Club, Edward, Prince of Wales. It was ten years before the hundreds of miles of pipes were completed.

Although greatly improved, the river was still far from clean. The sewage outflows were diverted downstream and until the 1900s they entered the Thames untreated. When the steamship *Princess Alice* sank in 1878, following a collision with the SS *Bywell Castle* during a moonlit voyage, it was the polluted water that many believe was responsible for the loss of some 700 lives. About an hour before the sinking, 75 million gallons of waste were released from the pumping station at Crossness and Barking, 'hissing like soda water with baneful gases so black that the water stained for miles'. It was reported that the bodies of the survivors and the dead were coated with a noxious slime that reappeared even when wiped away. Worse was still to come. In 1957, almost a hundred years since the Big Stink provoked outrage and action, researchers at the Natural History Museum declared the Thames to be biologically dead. Population increases, expansion and damage to infrastructure from wartime bombing meant the river was once more in a bad place. News reports described the Thames as an 'open sewer' with no oxygen in the water for miles either side of London Bridge. No fish could be found beneath its stinking, black surface.

The situation seems almost unthinkable now. The decline of riverside industries, coupled with the introduction of strict regulations about the dumping of effluent, mean the waters of the Thames have been completely revived. They are currently home to around 125 species of fish. Some 400 species of invertebrate can be found in its mud, water and river banks. The Thames is one of the world's cleanest city rivers. Sea lamprey and salmon – an indicator species when it comes to water quality – have both returned, while marine mammals, including seals, porpoises and dolphins, have all been spotted from the banks of Westminster. Even exotic and incredibly rare short-snouted seahorses have been found in the Thames, fanning their delicate bodies past Dagenham, Tilbury and Southend.

While the Thames will never be a natural river – it has been both narrowed and widened, walled and shuttered – the change in water quality means the river is once again a conduit of life, a wildlife superhighway that pulses through the very centre of London.

There is, of course, room for improvement. In 2017 Thames Water was fined £20.3 million after huge leaks of untreated sewage entered the Thames and its tributaries during 2013 and 2014. Furthermore, a combined sewage system means that flashes of heavy rain can still cause tens of millions of tonnes of untreated effluent to pour into the river each year, draining oxygen and killing fish. And littering, of course, continues to cause a problem.

Part of the solution, according to Chris Coode, the deputy chief executive of Thames21, a charity dedicated to improving London's waterways, is to heal the rift that has gradually developed between the Thames and those who live and work in the city, many of whom know enough of London's history to be aware of the river's troubled past. They associate the brown, the dirt of the natural fluvial estuarine sediment, with man-made grot. Couple the dark water with litter and it's not surprising people find it hard to see the life, the good, in the Thames. Citizen science projects, such as Thames River Watch, which focuses on the tidal Thames, are designed to introduce or reintroduce entire communities to the river and help them understand the relatively complicated workings of a city river. As Chris told me, 'All these people might care but not understand; once they understand, if we can convert them to being activists, they will be a powerful local voice for valuing and protecting the river.'

From Battersea, London really opens up. Only from the river is it really possible to see how the city is built around the Thames. The capital is a carapace; the houses, palaces and landmarks just so many sticks and stones in the river's caddis larvae case, almost crusting it over. Without the Thames there would be no London. Its dark waters have seeped into language, eroding consonants and forming banks of meaning, metaphor and poem. It is both landmark and locator. Londoners identify themselves in relation to its boundaries, whether they are north or south of the river. Under the red and yellow steel and granite deck arches of Vauxhall Bridge appears the sparkling rim of the London Eye on the south bank and, to the north, the sandy limestone of the Palace of Westminster.

As we creep forward more bridges unfold on the horizon, Lambeth, Westminster, Hungerford and Jubilee. We pull in just downstream of Vauxhall Bridge, under the MI6 building on the south bank. A police helicopter is flying up and downstream on a constant patrol, low enough for its rotors to send brown water scurrying to each bank. To our left a concrete slipway leads down from the road and onto the foreshore. As we unpack and strip from drysuits, a bright yellow amphibious vehicle, painted like a duck, trundles down into the river. Its passengers whoop as it makes a noisy transition from land to water, black smoke pumping from revving engine. It wobbles off, churning a diagonal path towards another slipway downstream on the north bank.

The foreshore is full of people walking with heads bent, eyes to the ground, occasionally stopping to pick something up, then casting it aside or placing it carefully in a bucket, basket or carrier bag. Modern mudlarks.* River scavengers. This hobby was once a way of life. During the eighteenth century, children as young as eight would search the foreshores of the Thames for anything of value – coal, old rope, rivets cast from ships – appearing as the tide fell, to earn their keep; it was a desperate, dirty, hand-to-mouth existence. Writing in 1851

* Mudlarking now requires a permit from the Port of London Authority.

in *London Labour and the London Poor; Extra Volume 1851*, Henry Mayhew described how mudlarks are mostly 'ragged, and in a very filthy state, and are a peculiar class, confined to the river. As soon as the tide is out they make their appearance, and remain till it comes in.' He also suggests that mudlarks did not necessarily wait for things to fall into the river and helped each other to knock coal from moored barges into the mud.

Keen to see what I can find, I walk away from the Pipe, where James is setting up the stove, and spot a thin, white clay pipe stem, nestled among chunks of ridged stoneware. There are nails too – mudlark gold – their flat heads rusted together to form skeletal knuckles. I pick a couple up and turn them over in my hand. Nearby is something bigger, also rusty. It's an ammunition clip. Five rifle bullets, the tips sharp as teeth, rusted into a clip that has held them for seventy years, the metal oxidised in copper greens, yellows and browns.

It's hard not to imagine back-stories to the finds. To think about the hands that held them and dropped them, only for the scouring tides of the Thames to return them decades or centuries on. I guess that's what draws people to the river now, fascination and curiosity rather than subsistence, to feel a tangible connection between changing worlds, all connected and shaped by the river. I turn the bullets and place my finger along their flesh-piercing tips. My grandad's last view of England as he departed for France in June 1944 was of the Thames. His ship steamed through London and moored off Southend before joining up with the Allied forces to liberate Europe. I imagine a soldier, young like him, standing on the deck smoking, his Enfield greased and slung over a shoulder. Twitchy. Fearful. Consumed by a panorama that he knows he may never see again. He probably didn't notice as the rounds slipped from his belt to clunk into the water. I hope he never needed them.

I head back to James and the Pipe again. I expected the river to be much busier. But apart from the revving *put-put* of the circling Duck, there aren't even any pleasure boats on the move. We're keen to get going, to push further into London. John MacGregor's most famous voyage began just a short distance from here. He described how the Rob Roy bounded away 'joyously on the top of the tide through Westminster Bridge . . . swiftly shooting Blackfriars' and danced 'along the waves of the Pool'. The water, he writes, was 'golden in the morning sun'.

I had hoped to reach his starting point, but the water is beginning to rise, the incoming tide rumpling the surface as the river slowly takes back its banks. The river may have transformed over decades and centuries, but it also does the same thing at least twice a day. The shifting water rebuilds and demolishes faster than any bank-side contractor. The river is never the same.

The action of the tide brings both challenges and benefits for the archaeologists who study this river. Projects such as Thames Discovery Programme (TDP) have been working along the river for a decade, trying to foster an understanding

of the Thames as an archaeological site and increase commu-
nity awareness about the structures and finds of the inter-tidal
zone. The water works with them and against them, the scour
and erosion uncovering new sites of interest, only to cover
them hours later. Fleeting and intriguing. Their fieldwork,
supported by English Heritage and the Museum of London,
uncovered London's oldest and probably least visited structure,
the remains of a prehistoric walkway whose wooden poles were
driven into the Thames, here at Vauxhall, some 6,000 years ago.
As we paddle away the tide is still low enough for us to see it
and even float through it, a relic of a culture of bone, stone and
wood; a time when fowlers, hunters and fishermen would have
camped alongside the wild, wide, marshy banks of the Thames.
We creep past. The wood, brown as iron. Dark as the river.

Behind the old walkway are signs of the tributaries that
once rushed to join the Thames. The River Effra, for example,
locked behind steel doors, with just the odd trickle allowed
to blend with the flow. The Thames has dozens of tributaries
along both its tidal and non-tidal course, but in the city many
have been forgotten or buried. The Fleet is the largest of these
subterranean rivers and was once a major flow. But, following
urban expansion, it was canalised and eventually disappeared
underground. Its mouth is now a drainage outlet in an embank-
ment wall under Blackfriars Bridge.

It's hard work going back upstream. Even with the tide,
the flow is strong and we stop for breaks, eking out the last of

the drinking water. James has brought along a new gadget for this trip – a gravity filter – but I've grumpily refused to use it, nervous of how effective it is, however clean the river is now.

We stop to rest opposite Battersea Power Station. The water is creeping up the stone beach, but there is still time to pad about. Scattered among river-scoured hag stones and the usual jetsam of the tide line are piles of bone, blackened by sediment and time. I can make out smashed femurs and ribs. Waste from old butcheries and tanneries, flushed from the sewers to form grisly drifts of bone mixed in with bits of pottery and masonry.

I walk over to them, picking shards up and feeling their weight, until I come across a jaw. Clearly belonging to a canid, it is much bigger than that of a fox; canines and molars still firmly rooted, chalky white against the blackness of the bone. My heart leaps. Could it be a wolf? A fragment of wildness offered up by the river; a relic of when lupine howls, not car alarms, would have cut through the night? It is about the right size and it has clearly been in the water for some time but I know it's unlikely. Wolves became extinct, or at least extremely rare, during the reign of Henry VII (1485–1509) and even then they were limited to the wild northern lands of Lancashire and Yorkshire. If the teeth of this jaw had been in the water for that long they too would have discoloured, scaled like a smoker's from the mud of the river. I weigh it again in my hand and stow it in the stern of the Pipe with my other treasures from the Thames.

I feel completely overawed by the Thames in a way I didn't expect. I knew that the sight of London from the water would be unique in terms of perspective – the city as a waterscape rather than a landscape – but this is something more. Perhaps it's because the Thames is such a busy, human river. It's the power of so many life stories converging on one point: a mess of spirits and song lines jostling for air time. I feel my own personal pull too, as if my trip has added another narrative to the millions that already make up the river's flow.

The wind is rising every hour, threatening to push the Pipe backwards. Although the tide is with us, it doesn't feel like it, with lumps of grey-brown water smacking into the bow and spraying over us. The eyots and bridges are no longer curiosities but obstacles that funnel the river against us, chopping the water into slapping mounds. By Fulham I'm exhausted. My shoulders ache from ruddering against the current and the rest of my body is stiff from straining forward, every muscle tired and taut. Along the bank to the right are long lines of people heading towards Craven Cottage football ground. A tribal gathering. It's match day. Further along, one fan enjoying a pint inside the ground leans over the river wall. 'Hurry it up boys; you're slower than our full-backs.'

We decide to take a final rest within earshot of the ground, listening to a hat-trick of groans from the home side. There is no dry land left now and we stand up to our ankles in water waiting for the kettle to boil. Without its banks the Thames looks transformed again. Broad and powerful, far removed from the non-tidal calmness at Teddington. This river, it feels, has come far – not just in terms of its journey from its source at Thames Head but in its use and abuse. But still it goes on. Still it endures.

James passes me a cup of tea and I sip it quietly, watching the water. He shoots me the odd look and raises an eyebrow before draining his mug with a satisfied and slightly theatrical sigh.

'What?' I ask.

'Tea OK, is it?'

'Yep . . .' I pause. 'I'm drinking the Thames, aren't I?'

CHAPTER 6

Tales of adventure

The trip is of the best possible kind: completely unplanned. Jen is off visiting family with the children and James is at a loose end. With forecasts promising spring sunshine, the pull of being on the water is simply too great. It's an opportunity to spend a couple of days messing about in the Pipe. The Granta, less than an hour's drive away, fits the bill. It has a reputation for fun. It overflows with the stuff. For decades, if not centuries, artists, writers, deepthinkers and atom-splitters have rowed, punted, bathed and swum in its soft, lazy waters, lolled and picnicked on its banks. After the labour and intensity of the Thames it also feels we need a bit of a break. This river will be, if not a holiday, an adventure of the Famous Five kind, albeit with a bit more rum in our ginger beer.

We have no idea how far we'll go. There is no end point, no destination. Ours is a map-less, watery wander, with little more than a canoe and a hammock. We will simply follow the river until we tire.

We put in on the mill cut, underneath a brick bridge topped with iron railings. The bank is butter-yellow with lesser celandine, drifts of petalled stars that slope gently to the water. On the opposite bank, behind a thick privet hedge, is a white house, its roof covered in wobbling red tiles. A sculpture of a horse, stark black against the soft greens, stands staring towards Cambridge, some two miles away. When the city's name developed in Middle English, changing from the Anglo-Saxon Grantebrycge, the river's name was altered to fit, becoming the Cam. But here, at least until Silver Bridge, it is still known as the Granta. A river draped with willows and catkins, its slow waters racing-green and powdered with pollen.

Our paddle strokes are glacier-paced and ponderous, the river rolls along next to lush water meadows. A path – the Grantchester Grind – skirts the bank, disappearing behind trees. Two runners, their lycra-skinned bottoms at our eye level, easily outpace the Pipe. Their progress down the river is marked by the metallic clink of kissing gates slamming shut. I don't bother ruddering to avoid the trees, instead gliding under willow fronds and ghosting round corners. A sunbather, as still as a corpse, lies by the bank, a towel covering his face and half of his chest. We pass within touching distance and James threatens to poke him with a paddle to check for signs of life.

A tight meander leads into woods, bringing relief from the high spring sun that has strobed the surface of the water. The river here smells sweet, perhaps from the grass and trees, the soft rot of vegetation or simply the water itself. I lie back and trail my fingers along the surface, watching them change colour as I plunge my hand in deeper. The water had felt thick and slow against the paddle, but against my skin it is light and silky; a soft, chilling balm. The light, filtered through the green lens of the tree branches and scrub, gives a sense of elvish twilight, even though it's barely noon. We drift and coo, lulled almost to sleep, to be startled awake by the sudden glare of sun on water or the froggy call of a moorhen, clattering away in fright.

It's hard not to get swept up in the sheer loveliness of it all. To get carried away. The poet Rupert Brooke, who lodged at Orchard House in Grantchester in 1909, never got over his time with the Granta. He kept the river with him, wound round his heart. Brooke's poem 'The Old Vicarage, Grantchester', written during his time in Berlin, is both satirical and deliriously nostalgic: a memory of 'flower-lulled' hours with water as 'green as a dream and deep as death'. More than a hundred years on, new happy memories are still being formed on the Granta. In among trees dripping with blossom, old branches have been lassoed with fraying rope swings that hang out over cool, dark pools, full of fish and fun. Our own laughter, our splashes and jokes, bounce from the banks, causing blackbirds to tut and scold.

The river straightens, becomes canalised as it runs into the city, a sluice draining the water down towards Silver Street Bridge. A concrete slipway, fitted with rollers, leads back down to the river, its flow looping round a willow-shaded green and the first colleges of Cambridge University. We lug the canoe up over the path, heaving with conga trains of tourists and then down the slope to the water. James hops in while I decide to give us a push-off. The water, though, is deeper than I was expecting. I step off the concrete and disappear with a startled shout, bobbing to the surface, still unable to touch the bottom. James takes the canoe back to the side, his shoulders shaking with laughter while I cling on grimly to the gunwales. On the path, two men, who appear to be dressed in Pikachu onesies, take pictures while shouting something in what sounds like Japanese. I give them a half-hearted wave, my teeth gritted. It's hard to keep hold of your sense of humour when you're being openly mocked by Pokémon.

I dry off while we eat lunch on the green, looking towards the putty-white Portland stone of the Silver Street Bridge, the marker of where the Granta becomes the Cam. Either side of the bridge is an armada of punts, their hardwood tills polished smooth by shuffling feet. Once used for fowling and trade, these are now crafts purely for pleasure: a means to transport tourists through the Backs – the famous stretch of the river where several colleges back onto the water. A few people are giving them a go, pricking nervously towards the bridge, while lunchtime drinkers, sitting in the gardens of the two riverside pubs, silently will them to fall in.

In the canoe again, we ease onto the Backs proper, a Hogwarts world of stone, brick and wood, dripping with history and stories. We slow down to watch some of the punts in action, their guides lowering wooden or aluminium poles into the river, pushing against the silty bed and then feeding them back through hand over hand. They talk as they go, a script learnt by heart and delivered in time with the rhythmic thrusts of the boat: the tales of a wooden bridge built by Newton (it wasn't); of disgruntled architects and controversial builds.

But there is fun to be had here too. More japes. Twice students have, for reasons known only to them, suspended cars from the Bridge of Sighs. In 1963, an Austin Seven was carried down the Cam on four punts before being strung up by ropes under the bridge. Five years later a Reliant Regal was left dangling from the bridge's structure, only to be removed the following morning by the long-suffering fire service. At King's College, students scaled the walls of the limestone chapel to place traffic cones – those luminous totems of student high jinks – on its spires. The college is said to have hired a scaffolding company the next morning to remove them but the job wasn't completed before nightfall. The climbers returned under cover of darkness, moving the cones to the back of the building and rendering the scaffolding pointless. Other items to have decorated the chapel spires include a toilet seat in 2002 and four Santa hats in 2009, all of which were retrieved at great expense (and I imagine little humour) by a professional steeplejack.

We drift slowly, the banks low and grass trimmed. It feels a bit like being on a fairground ride; a slow drift on a watery conveyor belt. By Midsummer Common, the punts make way for houseboats and we pass a parade of shuttered rowing clubs. The sun has now dipped behind thickening, porridge-coloured clouds and the wind has got up. A kayaker going upstream passes with a whir of blades, shouting out that 'It's easier this way.' The river is so straight it is numbing. We have the same view for what feels like hours, distant bridges and church towers not getting any closer no matter how hard we toil. The act of paddling is often soothing, the mind being lulled by the rhythm, but now it's hard work and with little to see I concentrate too much on my stroke. As soon as I think about it, I can't do it. I scrape my knuckles on the side, splash James's back or angle the blade so it gets little traction.

We break the tedium by tumbling from the canoe, floating like puffed-up starfish in our drysuits along the side of the bank, hooting and splashing at each other while cyclists and walkers do their best to ignore us. What was it Brooke said? 'For Cambridge people rarely smile, / Being urban, squat, and packed with guile.'

The day is drawing to a close. We're almost giving up on finding somewhere to camp when the river curves slightly to the east. On the right bank, nestling in the inner curve of the meander is a rough patch of land; a clump of old trees. A stream or an old drainage ditch runs horizontal to the river, circling the thicket like a moat, creating if not an island, then a woody peninsula. We paddle up it, away from the river's main flow, digging into silt that kicks up a rich, boggy, vegetable funk. The undergrowth is thick, scented with the peppery, pissy smell of nettle. Now only ankle-high, in a month or so they will make this place impenetrable – a fortress of spiked leaves and sting-ing hairs. The ground, though, is flat and dry.

I'm not sure of the time – it must be mid- to late-evening – but the sun has returned for a final hurrah. After seeming so grey, straight and . . . well, dull, on the last leg, the river is transformed. Everything trills and quivers in the sun. The water glows like iron fresh from the fire, solid yet malleable, soon to harden in the evening's cool. Even the mosquitoes and midges look beautiful: a living fog that rises and falls in the windless air towards water that has been smoothed to silk. A barn owl crosses the river and heads on silent wings for the neighbour-ing pasture, following the trees along the bank. I can feel the same calm and lightness I experienced this morning, a sighing peace that comes with the change of the land and the delicious, gradual slide of day into night. We are on the edge. Forgotten and close. In a bolt-hole that offers a thorny resistance to the pressures of agriculture. A place where the naiads can still hide, biding their time, before slipping back into the sparkling waters when the old magic of the evening returns – that between times on a river that is always between places.

I come to slowly, James is calling me. My hat is still pulled over my eyes and I nudge it up with my thumb. The light is pouring into my canvas cocoon, my body heating up with it. It feels late.

'What time is it mate?'

'About half ten . . . you've had a proper lie in.'

I can't work out where James's voice is coming from. I roll over, enjoying the bounce of the hammock, and unzip the side. James's gear has disappeared.

'Why didn't you wake me?' I say, swinging my legs over the side and searching for my boots with stockinged feet.

'I tried to. You told me to do one.'

I get up, rubbing the small of my back, stretching the sleep out of my arms and shoulders, and scan the camp for a sign of James.

His voice comes again. 'Be a love and pass me my tea.'

I look up. James is grinning like a Cheshire cat, perched some 25 feet up in the canopy. He scrambles down to a lower branch and I pass a tin mug up to him. Kicking his legs happily, he drinks it in the tree, shivelight illuminating his face like some woodland god. While I make breakfast and start to pack my own stuff, James descends from his roost and bounds off for a swim.

Through the arch of fallen ash I can just about see the river upstream, green and gilded gold by the sun. A squirrel scutters along the branch my hammock is still tied to, leaping over the bow knot and skittering up into the branches of a neighbouring tree, its tail flicking for balance while it chitters in annoyance. A chiffchaff is somewhere close. A bird I would probably struggle to recognise if I saw it, repeating its name with increasing enthusiasm. 'Chiffchaff, chiffchaff chiffchaff.' It's the two-tone beat of the changing season. 'Spring's here, spring's here, spring's here.'

Whether it is from spending so much time on rivers, or just because I'm getting older, I do feel like I have a keener appreciation of the rhythms and pulses of what's around me. I sense the ebb and flow of the seasons at a different level, the circles of life are tighter, more meaningful. And here, in a tiny, functioning fragment of woodland – no bigger than a thicket – that feeling is amplified and condensed. A microcosm of vibrant life, beautiful death and the wonder of change. Life and death on our little island.

We make good time returning to Grantchester, the river is busier with punts, rowing boats and kayaks. The houseboats are still moored but now there are people moving over them, tinkering and painting, watering potted plants and herb gardens.

There are even a couple of nudists on the bank in quieter sections, their skin piglet-pink against the greenery of the trees.

We've been swimming all the way along the route, ducking into the water in our drysuits to wallow and bob alongside the canoe, but I'm desperate for a proper swim, and so we're heading to Byron's Pool. Not counting our unplanned dunking in the upper Thames, it'll be the first of the year.

Now part of a local nature reserve, Byron's Pool takes its name from the most flamboyant of the Romantics, who Brooke suggested swam the pool – although whether he did or not will probably never be known. But Brooke himself certainly did bathe here and, aged twenty-four, invited Virginia Woolf to swim naked with him in the moon-dappled waters of the Granta. He no doubt entertained others there too. In his biography of Brooke's short but eventful life, *Rupert Brooke: Life, Death and Myth*, Nigel Jones suggests that Byron's Pool was also the location of the young poet's favourite party trick, a place where he 'jumped naked into the water and came up with an instant erection'.

Dominated by a large concrete weir, with a smaller stone weir to the left, the pool is now disappointingly unromantic. Above, the water may still be 'sweet and cool, / Gentle and brown', but below it is murky and unwelcoming. The foam from the weir's blackened discharge pipes congeals into a brown scum that collects round wooden jetties, now paced by fishermen rather than bohemian swimmers. Yellow signs stuck to the concrete and the iron railings warn against getting into the water. Roger Deakin abandoned the idea of swimming here, lamenting how 'the nymphs have departed and left no addresses', but even so, to see it for myself is a shock. What exactly was going through the minds of those responsible for building this?

Nevertheless, out of stubbornness and a desire to fulfil the only plan of the trip, I'm determined to swim. James and I strip to our boxers, leaving our clothes piled in the canoe, and run barefoot to one of the wooden platforms. The breeze against my unclothed skin is cold, and I know the longer I linger the harder it's going to be. There are people watching now too, suspicious of these strange men acting like kids. We count to three and jump, arms wrapped round knees tucked into our chests, a childish bomb – hardly an entry befitting a Romantic poet.

The point of immersion is always the moment when time stands still. First the splash, then the feeling of mud under feet, and then the rushing cold. It sucks away my breath, nerve endings scream as the skin contracts. We both break the surface gasping and laughing. The temptation is to climb out but instead I follow James as he strikes out for the weir, my skin flashing under the spittoon brown of the water. I go from a startled doggy paddle to breast stroke, frog-kicking first to the reeds on the right bank and then slowly round towards the willow. I porpoise clumsily, feeling the softness of the water through the chill.

As I move my chest feels warm, a kernel of heat born of adrenaline and joy. Under the willows I am shaded from the sun and as the wind skims the surface it goosepimples my flesh. James is still ahead of me, splashing out for the platform where we got in. He wriggles up it, slithering onto the wooden surface, and jumps up and down, whooping and flapping his arms to get the circulation going. I follow, slipping up the muddy bank, laughing. We flop out on the grass, lying in the sun to dry. My arms and legs are tingling, pulsing with the cold of the river. It feels like I have been jump-started, like I am utterly, truly alive.

It's Good Friday and my dad is driving us to somewhere where we can get the canoe onto the River Colne: a ford he used to run across during cross-country races at school. Head boy; long-jump record holder for a decade after he left; footballer; runner; Essex All Star. I don't ask when he last ran here. I don't want to turn that youthful vision to dust; to cause that memory of a teenage body in easy, carefree flight to seize up with bad knees and the lost yards that come with six and half decades.

For the first eighteen years of my life in Halstead the Colne cut through everything. A gorgeous emerald-green river, glimpsed through wrought-iron railings, glugging under the grand, white-boarded front of the old mill. It is the river of my childhood, a place that has shaped my memory and my identity. I cycled upstream with my brother to fish and, closer to home, walked through fields, then empty of houses, to play with friends on its banks and in its cool waters. The Colne, or, as we called it then, the river (after all there was no other river), was a favourite haunt. We would shed shoes and socks and wince our way through cold water and sharp stones. It was a place of endless summer, where the sun would burn our necks and bounce from the water to redden faces. The river was a refuge, an edgeland of almost otherworldly remoteness, even though we could see the wooden fences of the new estate through the trees; could smell the creosote, taste the barbecues and hear the stop-start hum of lawnmowers on the other side.

The water offered an education too, in meanders and flows, fish and insects – and in the birds and the bees. A sodden magazine rescued from the black waste pipes that crossed the river gave me my first, and slightly horror-filled, glimpse of open-legged nakedness. It was from the Colne that I ran hand in hand with a girl, stealing a kiss in a cornfield wet from a sudden shower, the wheat whipping against river-cold legs. Our lips locked for electrifying seconds before we darted back to the water and our friends, who eyed us with cool suspicion, as if they noticed a change in dynamics; a slight thawing of innocence.

I would still return to the river when I was older. As a teenager I sat on my bike by Parsons Bridge to watch the water flow away, wishing I could join it and escape too. And eventually I did, moving away to Brighton for twelve years. During that time I met my wife and became a father of two children myself. It was probably only then that I felt East Anglia's unexpected pull, a dull yearning for wide skies and the closeness of family. The river, listless in its small valley, calling me home again.

My dad, though, has never spent a winter away from this catchment. Born in Sible Hedingham, not far from where the river's source converges at Great Yeldham, he married a school-boy crush from a village downstream that took the river's name, Earls Colne. From the back-bedroom window of my family home in Halstead you can see the river, or at least the trees that mark its slow passage through the outskirts of the town. Occasionally my parents talk of moving away; of going west or south; but I don't see it. Their movements around this valley are as habitual and as worn as the river. Part of me thinks it would be too much of a wrench to leave somewhere that is so well known and well trod. The family roots are just too deep in the silt of the Colne.

The water is shallow but moving nicely, the river young and lively. The sky is a bright white with a darkening grey smudge to the east that suggests Bank Holiday rain. Along the scal-loped banks the first hint of blossom is starting to show, white marshmallow balls of budding hawthorn blossom, willow cat-kins swelling from bud scales. The odd scrap of fleece, blown from where a shepherd was shearing his flock at the ford, clings to stones and sticks, waxy with lanolin. We hop in and out of the canoe, often managing little more than ten shallow strokes before the Pipe grinds to a halt against the river bed.

I think James is wondering why I've brought him here. There are so many other rivers we could have gone to; ones deep enough to paddle. Part of it is sheer bloody-mindedness. As with the Lark, I've been told you can't canoe here. Despite its historic navigation the river has become 'private'. The free water now 'owned'. I've also been warned of trees blocking the way, of barbed wire that laces across its flow. The umpteen 'You'll never get throughs' are like red rags.

James has told me before that our travels often remind him of the David Lynch film *The Straight Story*, an account of a man's journey across the heartland of America on a ride-on lawnmower. I know exactly what he means. Not only is our speed and naivety matched, but I remember getting the same feeling watching that film as I do whenever we set out in the Pipe. It is a sense of freedom about being able to make our own way, coupled with a slight sense of the ridiculous and just a hint of obstinacy: 'We will do it this way even if it kills us.'

And I think James also understands I had to come here, to see somewhere that's been a geographical constant in my life. This is my river.

The route of the water wiggles constantly like it's trying to shake us off. The bank is high, but after the ford, the river feels more like a ditch, a drainage channel that has little room to breathe. With no landmarks visible I'm finding it hard to tell where we are, but we can't have gone far. Another flow, another drain, joins the Colne just before we pass under the stomach-flipping hump of the bridge that carries the road to Castle Hedingham and my dad's old school.

On the way here he told us that he used to raft down this river nearly every summer, setting out from Alderford Mill downstream to this very bridge. Aged just ten or eleven, he and his friends, Steve, Michael, Peter, Tom (he rattles off the names as if it were yesterday), would spend two days lashing together logs, timber and 45-gallon oil drums nicked from Steve's dad's garage, before stowing their craft in among the trees. They would meet again at first light – my dad creeping from his house as his father left for work at the dairy – to spend long days going up and down the river, only to return for dinner, sodden, grimy, sunburnt and happy. Almost the whole village would be by the water's edge, swimming, paddling, fishing.

He tells me they used to play a *Swallows and Amazons* game of cat-and-mouse with the Water Board too, who would commandeer their craft to clear the water of weeds and fallen trees, leaving it on the bank somewhere up the river when they were finished. The boys would respond in kind, waiting for the long shadows of twilight before taking the Water Authority's own flat-bottomed skiff and hiding it among the trees. I'm glad he's shared the story now. I'm used to the company of Deakin, Stevenson and MacGregor on these trips, but it feels good to have my dad at my shoulder, a young ghost of summer's past to warm a grey spring day.

I doubt my dad or the rest of his gang would recognise their river now. A raft would struggle with the river's width, and there's little evidence of anyone clearing anything from this river. A few willows have exploded from the bank, dragging their branches into the water, while nettles – already taller and broader than their Cam cousins – marshal both sides. The water is so shallow that the dorsal fins of fish, flitting past us in flickering brown shoals, break the surface as they force their way upstream. They disappear in a silvery puff of bubbles, oxygen squeezed through blood-red gills.

We stop to make tea beside Alderford Water Mill, taking photos of the mill's white clapboard walls, which reflect off the river's surface. The Colne, described even by those who love it as 'short and undramatic', was once busy with industry. The Domesday Book records thirty-three mills working along its length between Great Yeldham and its mouth at Point Clear, past Brightlingsea, where it empties into the North Sea. There were once some even further upstream than here, but they have long since been swept away by evolving industry. Thankfully Alderford Mill was saved. Bought in 1994 by Essex County Council, it has been restored with the help of the Friends of

Alderford Mill. I've heard that when the water levels allow, the wheel still turns, but no longer do the stones it drives have any real purpose. It is a ghost of a machine.

I walk back to James and help him haul the Pipe up and round the sluice. We place her scraped bottom on a concrete block that runs from beneath the gates, hoping the small flow of water will give us a push over. It doesn't. We gamely sit rocking back and forward, before giving up and pushing the canoe into the deeper water.

From the mill, the river curves in a gentle crescent, wooded and peaceful. Quite a few trees have fallen into the water. Some we can ease our way past, the canoe's painted sides squeaking against the scratching branches, while others we chop through with a hatchet. The further we go the more clogged the river becomes, forcing us onto the nettle-guarded banks to get past. Even the water, sluggish and thick against the paddles, is hesitant to let us through. The blockages create curdled mats of weed and wood; a slimy, ectoplasmic gunk that coats paddles and clings to our legs when we get out.

It takes us a good hour to reach the next mill. Although, as the crow flies, the distance is not much more than a mile, the bends of the river mean we have probably done three times that. We drag the canoe over to a shallow ford to avoid portaging across what is now someone's garden. A woman, presumably the current owner of the mill, takes a break from unloading shopping from a car and walks over. She says she has often paddled upstream with her daughter in an inflatable boat, but the downed trees and low water have meant it's been impossible for much of the year.

Her husband comes to join her and offers to open the mill's sluice for fifteen minutes to give us 'a fighting chance of getting through'.

We thank them and load up quickly while they go off to open the sluice, cranking the rusting handle. The water rises quickly, swirling and buffeting round the Pipe.

'You won't have long,' the woman shouts, 'so go as fast as you can.'

The Pipe rushes and bobbles on the new flow, the paddles no longer raking the bottom but forming clean strokes as we race to keep up with the river. The cut is narrow and the water, with nowhere to go, keeps its speed, creating a creamy wave that never breaks. I hear a voice and look up. The woman's daughter is running alongside us on the bank. Aged ten or eleven, probably the same age as my dad when he rafted on the Colne, her legs and arms are pumping to get ahead of us, shouting a warning about a toppled tree further downstream but mostly just following the river: chasing us, chasing the water.

The river squeezes out of the trees and back into farmland, first put to arable and then grazing. The grass has been nibbled short and the banks retreat away from us; still steep but hoof-hit and foot-fretted, they have turned to sandy dust. Another oak has fallen horizontally across the river and we stop again, this time unpacking the stove for tea and a late lunch.

I scramble up the bank to try and see where we are, my feet sending up smoke signals of dust. I don't quite believe it. Just 100 feet away is the main Hedingham Road, a road I have travelled endlessly both as a passenger – staring out of the rear window on the way to and from my dad's old house, where my grandparents still live – and then later as a driver. I never realised the river was here; sunken in this field, unmarked, unnoticed. I guess before I started these voyages I had no idea where the Colne came from or went to. For me it was always an isolated river. The only river. An oxbow lake of my imagination.

James pokes a paddle towards something emerging from the bottom of the river. The bed and the banks look like they are covered in brightly coloured clams, thick lips sealed and pushed through the silt.

'What is that?'

He jabs at it again, dislodging it with a swirl of mud and flicking it into the Pipe. It's a clay pigeon. They form stacks almost a foot deep, toxic orange and milk-white, a clutter of blasted fragments and cowering missed prey. James gouges another out of the river bed.

'They're everywhere. Jesus Christ what a mess.'

If anything, the grass on the banks is even worse. Among the shattered clays, plastic cartridge cases lie in transparent drifts, thousands of them, their lead shot spent and sprayed across land and water. We try and put them in the canoe, but there are just too many, the whole surface of the river is filmed and bubbled with plastic. Drifting and choking. It will take decades for this plastic to break down, but even then it won't entirely disappear; it will just grow less visible, entering the food chain to cause a creeping, slow death. It's a maddening, disgusting mess. The same landowners who want to bar access from the waterways treat them with casual, callous disregard.

The river emerges from trees and swings east. The right bank slowly grows in height and turns into the man-made grassy wall that leads round to the concrete mouth of Halstead's floodgates. I was living in Brighton on 21 October 2001, when an entire month's rain fell on Halstead in the space of a single day. As the rain came down the waters came up. The swollen Colne burst its banks and inundated houses for the first time in more than fifty years. In the centre of town, the water crept over the High Street bridge, leaving pavements more than a foot and a half underwater. Those who didn't leave their houses described how they had tried in vain to scoop away the water as it bubbled through floorboards and doors. But it was only when the rain eased that the flood retreated, leaving homes mud-caked and ruined, slimed and slick with the river's breath.

These floodgates are part of the solution. Under normal conditions water passes through them, but if the level rises special sensors automatically adjust the gates to control the volume of water passing through. Should such a flood come calling again, the gates will close completely, creating a temporary lake behind them – presumably reaching to the top of the grass bund. The whole project, opened in 2006, cost around £4 million. I'm sure those affected by the last flooding will think they are worth every penny. But the gates, like every modern sluice or weir I've come across on the river, are excessively ugly.

The concrete, blackened by perpetual damp, is wedged into the earth and edged with dull steel railings. It is a Mad Max fortress, devoid of joy, just like the one at Byron's Pool. The doors themselves hang open like a trap, leading into a dark, grotty concrete corridor. The water is full of brown weed that look like clumps of hair in a plughole and clinks with discarded beer bottles. We hold our breath and paddle through. It's almost completely black, the walls are slimy to the touch and the air is strangely cold, tanged with iron.

Whoever designed this monster also hated canoeists. Coming out of the tunnel we encounter two rows of concrete teeth, set just far enough apart to make it seem that navigation is possible, but close enough to each other to take fist-sized splinters out of a boat. Sticks, weeds, more bottles, balloon scraps, a flip-flop and a condom are all stuck on them too. We get out, levering the Pipe through, slipping and sliding up to our thighs in reeking, unidentifiable grot.

The floodgates have altered the landscape but I'm sure this is Box Mill, named after the two flour mills – now long gone – that once stood here. A lot has changed since I used to come here with my brother some twenty-five years ago. The land is no longer grazed by sheep and nettles and scrub have moved in and covered it, closing the gaps in the trees. The river itself is almost completely shaded, a watery holloway.

These trips were partly about expanding my psycho-geography, but here, seen from the canoe, it feels like my world has shrunk. Yes, the landmarks are as I remember them: the grey veteran oak, the halfway marker for my own school cross-country runs; the iron bridge where we played Pooh sticks; the old bollard still at its entrance, green with age, its curved top polished by a century of passing hands. But now they are all flung together in a chaotic closeness, both familiar and strange; my childhood haven has become small and pinched.

To the left, through the arching loops of willow, there is movement. A little owl flies across the river, its rounded wings beating ten to the dozen. It settles in a standard oak, my cross-country tree, bobbing its head up and down, and fixes us with a fierce, piercing stare. I stop paddling to watch, taking in its broad head and puffed-up plumage; brown and pale buff, streaked and speckled like ruffled tweed. There is something scholarly about little owls. The way they run along the ground after prey, like an irritated schoolmaster on his way to mete out punishment to some ne'er-do-well.

The water continually shallows and deepens by turns as we approach Rosemary Lane football ground, whose floodlights crane above a green corrugated-iron fence that is patched and buckled, its upper edge nibbled and moth-holed by rust. The industrial estate, home to the new industries that replaced the old, still clings to the river. I remember when this whole place smelt new, visiting every other weekend to pick up films from the video shop, a rotation of *Ghostbusters* and *Star Wars*. The place looks tired now and, again, smaller.

Screened by trees, the river turns once more towards the town. An alder has fallen into the water and a willow, also toppled but still growing, has helped create a dam of sticks, weed, mud and rubbish. The water has stopped moving, forming a kidney-shaped, almost stagnant bowl. The surface has a thick tobacco-spit-brown skin that wrinkles with the paddles, the water being too thick to whorl.

We would normally try and stay in the river to guide the canoe past the branches, but neither of us wants to go in here. James jumps to the bank and I slip and slide after him, a trailing leg landing in the water and emerging covered in snotty gloop with a smell of fermented death.

We head under the High Street bridge and onto the Causeway, a canalised section that feeds into Townsford Mill. I can't remember ever seeing the water so low. Waste pipes from the houses that line the Causeway have been exposed. They span the entire width of the river. Some are above our head, while others are lower and ominously warm to the touch as we clamber over, dragging the canoe behind. Beaches have formed on either side of the river and long, grey, stony bars, already covered in grass, rise from the water in the middle. Even the ducks I used to feed as a child have had enough and moved onto wetter, more attractive hunting grounds.

Two or three people have gathered to look at the canoe, leaning over the railings to get a better view of the eccentrics walking down their river. A couple of teenage girls, hair pulled facelift-tight, point and giggle at us as we splosh downstream.

There is a concern in the town that the river is at risk of emptying and a sense of deep frustration that it hasn't been resolved. What little water there is still filters into the mill, sliding down a brick-lined tube that once led to the giant waterwheel. I remember coming on school trips here, a short walk from my old primary. Two or three children invariably threw pencils or note pads into the water and then we would all rush into the mill's viewing gallery to watch them rotate and mulch in the slatted fury of the wheel.

We slither over the sluice, the water barely an inch deep over bricks matted with spongy green algae. Both James and I are thinking the same thing: could we get the Pipe through?

'Do you think the wheel is still down here?' I ask James.

He cocks his head to one side and then tries to walk a bit further on, skating over weed.

'Well, it's not turning if it is. It's silent down there.'

We walk back up and collect old bricks and stones, stacking them on one side of the broken sluice gate. It's a crude dam but it does the job; the depth of the water is already increasing and the Pipe is tugging at its painter, ready to rush into the soggy subterranean. We position the canoe's bow towards the narrow opening, running forward with it like a bobsleigh and jumping in at the last moment. The Pipe rushes up the wall on the outside bend and then swings back the other way, gathering speed as it goes. Paddles are useless. Instead we kneel and brace, tucking our arms and heads in, feeling the joins of the bricks rippling through the bottom of the canoe.

There's a moment when I worry that the wheel may still be there, that this brick-lined hell mouth will deliver us to our Maker – splintering the canoe and crunching bone. We pop out into darkness, a man-made cave with dripping ceilings and a smell of damp and cold. Our shouts bounce off the walls. It takes a few moments to adjust to the gloom; we paddle forward, the water is deep and its sound is emphasised and echoing, joining the plops from the ceiling and the steady trickle from the tunnel behind us.

Outside the mill the depth goes again and we get out, dragging the canoe under the bridge next to the old metal works. I don't know if it's still running. I remember the smell of it though, sweet like burnt vegetables. I used to linger here to breathe it in and watch the pike that often hung in the waters below. It's too low for pike now; there's just an egret, up to its ankles, dagger-beaked and stalking. We return to walking, splashing towards the road bridge, through brown weeds that flow underwater like dirty hair.

Across the road, near the fire station with its Trumpton-red doors, the land has been given over to a nature reserve. A walkway follows the river, dotted with benches and wooden jetties for pond-dipping and play. The water is deep enough to paddle and we zip along, chased by a young girl on a bike, her stabilisers bouncing off stones and tree roots. The sun is starting to come out, turning the puddle brown of the water to a light khaki green. The river quietens again and houses appear by the left bank, their backs to the Colne. The string of fences looks familiar; older, faded, bowing and rupturing in places, but this is it, the edgeland of my youth.

We stop and I take off my boots to paddle, inching over stones that dig into the arches of my bare feet. The water is ice-cold, clear again. In many ways, it feels odd to have returned here. I don't know what I expected to find. I suppose that, for me, the Colne has always been a river of lost summers. In some ways these journeys are about recapturing that sense of childhood joy and freedom. But I wonder if my memories of the Colne have been polished to an unnatural shine by the passage of time. Perhaps I expected all those summers still to be in the water, pinned against a log jam or a new weir. I can't help but feel sad, pricked by nostalgia. But no, that word doesn't really cover it. The Welsh have a better one: 'hiraeth', a longing for a home to which you cannot return. A grief for a lost youth. The writer Katharine Norbury has suggested another word: 'Sehnsucht'. Less grief, more yearning. It can apply to a place or a time one has never really known. Perhaps some secret windows can't, or shouldn't, be opened for a second time.

I climb the bank to dry my feet. But I am glad I came here. It feels like some kind of circle has been completed. Change, both in me and the river, has been confirmed. I take one last, long look before we set off. I know I'll probably never come back again. I couldn't if I tried.

CHAPTER 7

River seekers

We follow the rat runs created by dogs and fishermen down the bank, slipping with the canoe onto our arses and coming to a juddering stop by the water's edge. The river rolls from under Hereford's Wye Bridge like scalded milk, the whorls that spread across its surface are as big as dinner plates. The Wye. It couldn't be more different from our last river, the Colne. Its flow is broad and powerful; it's the fifth-longest river in the UK, stretching and twisting 134 miles from its source at Plynlimon in the Cambrian Mountains to reach its sister, the Severn. The Wye, or in Latin 'Vaga', meaning wandering. Its Welsh name, 'Gwy', perhaps rooted in 'Gwybiol' or 'Gwyr', has a similar sense, along the lines of crooked, wandering hills. They are old names for an old river; a river that hasn't lost its magic, its stories, its sense of adventure. Perfect for riparian thrill-seekers.

This waterway was once busy with trade. Iron, coal, lumber,

wheat and flour, wool and cider were hauled and sailed in barges and trows. There were even said to be pirates on the river: men and women who waited in the shadows of the Forest of Dean to board barges and remove bushels of corn. A lawless river, gloriously free.

The Wye lives up to its name; it is a place of wandering, of pleasure. With an undisputed right of navigation extending from Hay Town Bridge all the way to the Severn Estuary at Chepstow, it is one of the most popular destinations in the UK to canoe and row. I've been told it is a paddler's dream: a beautiful river with meandering and tumbling waters that flow through wooded valleys and limestone gorges, enjoyed by everyone from beginners to seasoned canoeists and kayakers.

We push off into water that is just deep enough for a full stroke, not that it's needed. The river carries us away from the town, running over flat rocks with the sound of polite applause. Sunday afternoon at the cricket. It's hard not to be hypnotised by the constant movement of the water. The surface rucks and rumples round stones; froths, hiccups and foams over gentle rapids that don't so much as rock the Pipe, but lift and carry her over with an 'On your way, on your way.' The patterns on the water's surface are a map of the bed, the wrinkles and eddies, contours of rocks and sunken branches that change the flow even if they are deep enough not to scrape the canoe.

On the east bank the ground rises quickly to form a steep, wooded slope. Houses sit at the top, perched on stilts, flights of stairs traipsing down gardens that lead down to the river. The water level is high, bolstered by Welsh rain and tributaries, but the trees, flagged with rags and cluttered with river-crafted walls of wattle and daub, show it has been higher still. The sun, hidden behind clouds for most of the long drive from Suffolk, now winks between the trees, green and gold, bouncing off the water with a light like a Bonfire-night sparkler.

The warmth of the afternoon has brought other life to the river. The air is full of tiny wings. At first I think they are moths who have finally given up on the dim light of the moon. But these are caddis flies. They hang in dense, fluttering clouds, a brown, wind-blown blizzard, dipping back to the water from where they have sprung before drifting upstream on the breeze. There are so many that we have to paddle with our mouths closed, picking them from our hair and clothes while using our paddles to rescue those that fly too close to the water.

The river turns, heading south-west, and we come to a series of rocky steps that create a bulge of green, sun-scalded water: a river roller that pushes the Pipe on like the jerking contraptions of a theme-park log flume. A gentle thrill.

The far bank is awash with colour: explosions of linen-white blossom, cherry, a May mess of hawthorn mixed with candyfloss pinks, all set against the soft ochre of sandstone and the green of hard bud and leaves. There are so many greens. Hundreds. It feels like there should be more words: for the yellow-tinged green of the old grass by the water's edge; the lighter green of new grass and meadow; the wine-bottle green in the jagged hearts of nettle leaves and flowerless plants; the darker shades of the small thorns, moss and fern, the ivy-draped oak trunks and pine. Peppermint, emerald, gentlemen's club, old welly, bin juice, toad's back. Small fish dart under the Pipe, clearly visible in the shallows, while in the deeper pools their bigger cousins glide against the current, their backs moony white.

We make camp on a small floodplain of water-smoothed mud on the east bank, which sweeps up to a bund separating the river from a farmer's field and hiding us from view. Watching the river, both here and in the canoe, I have had a real sense of how the Wye fills the valley, or, rather, of how it made the valley. Millions of years of water on rock, of freeze and thaw. Laid out in this valley is not just a river of this time, but of all times. These trips, my life, are shorter and dimmer than a match flame against the grinding, scouring geological processes that have made this riverscape. It is something that is too much to really comprehend, or hold onto. It comes in quick, startling, lightning flashes that are almost like pulses of adrenaline. Perhaps this is also what draws people to this river, or any river.

For James, this is already his favourite trip. The lively water, the wooded slopes have brought a sense of excitement and adventure that he didn't get on the Colne. It's the kind of place he imagined when we first discussed exploring with the Pipe: a wide river that rolls endlessly on, full of joy, beauty and possibilities. We cook over the naked flames and then sit and talk until the last log burns down to a dull red heat, watching the dark rush down the valley sides, across the river and into our camp like ink bleeding across a page.

When the water is still and the sky bright, it can sometimes feel as if you're neither of the land nor the water. Floating through a reflective world, it is like flying through branches and cloud. But now we really are going through cloud. The river banks are quietened and muffled by a dripping blanket of ground-scraping fog that clings to us and the canoe. The sun burns, a lighter, brighter disc in a wall of white. The fog is thicker than the pea-souper on the Thames, another ghostly flow that mirrors the water's path. It's impossible to see where we're going, so we paddle slowly in the middle of the river, mindful of rocks and fishermen making the most of an early start.

We can hear the sound of white water ahead and slow the Pipe, drifting into the bank and walking along sharp, sand-coloured stone to get a view of what is in front of us. A line of water, humping and frothing, stretches from the west bank on our right to an island, straggled with young willow and scrub. A few Canada geese slap about on black paddled feet, while further back I can make out two or three others sitting on nests. To the left of the island the water is calmer, possibly deeper, although the current is faster as the river rushes past the obstruction.

Rapids, even a Grade-1 – the kind that seasoned kayakers and canoeists wouldn't get out of bed for – are still a novelty for us, so we decide to go right. We return to the Pipe and head for a point where the submerged rocks look flatter and easier to navigate. The bottom of the canoe ripples as we glide over, rushing past the geese who ruffle their wings, honking and hissing with territorial indignation.

There is more than one island. It's a muddy archipelago, a gravel bar that has grown with sediment and time. If it weren't for the geese, which I doubt would have tolerated the company, this would have been a perfect camping spot. The water calms to a whisper but we can hear the sound of another rapid on the other side. We both stand in the canoe, trying to see what we're missing out on, the Pipe wobbling precariously but continuing its glide downstream.

Not far on a fisherman, the first we have seen on the Wye, is standing in the middle of the river, braced against the flow. He uses his left hand to feed the line back towards him with gentle downward strokes, then flicks the rod in front of him, the gossamer trail of line cast out, looping, then rushing forward, the fly landing on the water's surface and spinning immediately with the current. He does it again and again, waiting for the fish to rise and bite, to break their hunger strike and give into snapping instinct.

The Wye is famous for its salmon, particularly the spring salmon that have spent three or more years at sea before returning to spawn, often in their natal river. On reaching the river estuary salmon undergo physiological and morphological changes. As salinity decreases, sperm and egg production increase and the salmon's reliance on the red muscles that have powered it through the sea switches to the white muscles used for bursts of speed and jumping; the slow-twitch muscles of the endurance runner make way for the bulging fast-twitch of the sprinter. Its colour changes too, darkening and losing the silver sheen that confuses ocean predators. The male, a cock or buck, develops canines and a hump, its jaws growing into a pronounced curve or kype. A fish-hook of its very own.

The spring salmon, which enter the Wye between January and June, have been known to reach extraordinary sizes. The largest recorded was caught by Doreen Davey in March 1923. She had been fishing from the Cowpond Pool at Ballingham, not far, I think, from where we camped last night. It took one hour and fifty-five minutes for her to land the fish, darkness falling by the time she wrestled it onto the bank. I've seen a picture of her online, standing stony-faced in a long, pleated skirt and woollen sweater, hair tucked inside a broad-brimmed hat. Hanging beside her from a wooden A-frame is a giant fish, as long as her body and as wide as her waist. There have, of course, been tales of other, bigger fish on the Wye. The ones that got away. One dead fish found rotting on the foreshore was estimated to weigh 80 pounds.

The number of salmon in the Wye has fallen dramatically over the last century. In 1967 the rod catch was 7,864; by 2002 it was just 357. It has taken hard work to bring the numbers back up, to identify and address a catalogue of problems: blockages that prevented migration; sheep dip; excessive grazing that had widened the flow; overshadowing from uncoppiced trees and in places a pH level that was only a little less acidic than vinegar. According to the Wye and Usk Foundation, 2016 saw a two-decade high in catch numbers, with more than 500 salmon caught by registered anglers.

Round the next meander there are more fishermen. Standing up to their waists in the river, they form a long diagonal line, a dot-to-dot of cast and lure, quietly hoping to flash their fly under the nose of a fish. It's nice to see them in the water rather than hunched on the banks. Here they are more immersed in their surroundings, the river pushing into the backs of their knees. They seem cheerier for it; chatting and laughing as we slow to talk or ask them which side we should go. The Wye is a place of adventure for them too. Like paddlers, they are drawn here for the beauty of the water and the thrill of their sport, the chance to hook a trout, a grayling, perhaps even a salmon.

In the past there has been conflict between paddlers and anglers on the Wye. Complaints have been lodged to the police by both sides. Maybe there is a rogue fisherman who resents the free access to a waterway for which he has paid, or an over-zealous bailiff. I can also see how a large group of paddlers – a stag group weighed down by beer and hangovers – would irritate even the gentlest soul. But here and now, as we paddle quietly past three fishermen, their lines arching and falling, a loop of cast and lure, it is harmony. Like windmills on the Sussex Downs, the anglers add something.

The morning is a pure delight. The sun is high and hot, making up for lost time. It bounces from the water, scolding our half-closed eyes. Through squinted eyes the river is bronze, like a trace of moth scales floating on the water. I can feel my skin heating up, my face tightening.

We lunch at Foy, skidding over a white lip of water to pull onto an island that overlooks a church on the north bank. It stands on a small ridge of exposed red sandstone, the river wrapping round it to create a sheep-grazed peninsula. Sand martins wriggle out of their bank-side burrows as if they were a pair of tight jeans, to swoop and make sharp turns above the water. Their tails are like the vanes of an arrow, nocked and shot from a bow.

I decide to swim, stripping down to my boxers and walk-ing out into water that chills my legs and sends a delicious shudder running up to my shoulders. I dip down onto my haunches to let the water hit my chest, gasping with shock but glad to get the point of immersion over. Although the water is shallow, where the river splits to go round the island the flow has scoured the bed to a greater depth. The strength of the current means that if I swim hard enough I can just hang in the water, the river becomes an endless pool. James joins me and we launch ourselves at the flow again, splashing, laughing and gulping in water, before giving in and flopping onto our backs to float downstream.

Swimming in the river has its own thrills; the senses are heightened and deepened. But occasionally it also has its dangers. Especially, it would seem, here. I've heard it said that the Wye is a 'hungry river' that demands one life each year. The price of beauty is high.

Close to where we started at Hereford stands a stone memorial that also serves as a warning. Chipped into the granite are the words: 'In memory of Scott Trout and all of those who lost their lives in the River Wye. Don't let it be you.' Downstream another stone, erected two centuries earlier, to the memory of sixteen-year-old John Whitehead Warre, stands 'to warn parents and others to be careful how they trust the deceitful stream'. It concludes: 'God preserve you, and yours from such calamity.'

I wonder if it is the undercurrent of danger that attracts people to the river just as much as its beauty, or the coolness of its waters. The bridge-jumper, the tomb-stoner, the daredevil, the show-off, even the all-season swimmer, sense something else when they break the surface: their mortality.

Ross-on-Wye is easily the busiest place we've been on a river outside of London. The waterside pubs are heaving: tourists and locals alike are drawn to the banks by the weekend sun. This part of the Wye Valley has been a destination for centuries. In fact, Ross is often described as the birthplace of package tourism. In the late eighteenth and early nineteenth centuries, people would tour the valley by boat, enjoying the views of the wooded banks, the craggy lookouts and the serpentine course of the river itself. Dr John Egerton, a rector from Ross-on-Wye, was said to be the first person to build a craft especially for visitors to explore the Wye. Other boats soon followed, carrying the well-heeled, along with artists, writers and poets. Wordsworth, Turner, Philippe de Loutherbourg, Michael 'Angelo' Rooker, Coleridge and Thackeray all took inspiration from the river.

Most of them would have come to the Wye Tour with a copy of *Observations on the River Wye, and Several Parts of South Wales* by William Gilpin, written in 1770 about his journey by boat from Ross-on-Wye to Monmouth. A pioneer of the Picturesque, Gilpin believed it was up to the artist to modify nature to make a good picture, to master the wild, to correct and improve it. He took an engaging landscape and waterscape and boiled them down to a disinterested view that misses the true joy of experiencing wild spaces: being part of them.

We press on. To our left, on the east bank, fields still domi-
nate the landscape, furrows of brown that lead away from the
water. But to the right, the trees have returned. The valley side is
covered with dense walls of pine, sweeping down to a limestone
boulder-strewn, mossy foreshore. More thick woods follow,
deep green and shading the water, branches reaching out to
the Pipe. I watch their reflections break with the motion of the
canoe and the slow churn of the paddles, only to gather again
as soon as we've passed. It's like a mirror un-smashing.

Twice we stop to see if we can camp but both times the
spots are too close to a path and much steeper than we thought;
I fear we'll roll out of our hammocks and into the river. There
is also a darkness among the trees that I find unsettling. No
light enters through the closed canopy. The pleasant smell of
crushed needles is outweighed by a heavy stillness, a pregnant
pause that heralds terror. Nothing moves, nothing lives under
the trees. I feel silly but ask James if we can keep going.

A gentle, tree-fringed gravel beach on the west bank
looks like an ideal campsite, but as we get closer I can see a
'No-landing' sign has been hammered into the mud. About
four or five miles away from Ross-on-Wye the trees to our right
shrink back around what looks like an old deer park and the
ruins of Goodrich Castle. It dominates the river, though it's not
close enough to be reflected in the water. Instead the building
mirrors the land that surrounds it, its rounded bricks echoing the pale sandstone it stands on. We stop nearby but as we

make space for our hammocks, find that rolls of barbed wire have been left to rust, their toothy loops waiting to snare our legs and arms. We keep going. A group of teens watches us bob over rapids, their conversation falling as they wait to see if we'll make it. We paddle now in silence, the light softening and shading to a twilight gloom. My arms and hands are aching and my sunburnt face is kicking out a pricking heat, my own breath hot as the temperature falls. I've given up looking to the bank but James sees a sign half submerged in the water.

'Stop here for ice-cream.' We spin the canoe and head for a landing platform where two other canoes are hidden behind trees. It's the riverside entrance to a youth hostel. I slop up the steps and head for the reception.

We string our hammocks up at the edge of the field. The woods slope steeply up, the ground covered with bluebells. The mud, baked dry, is full of deer slots and just ten feet away a fallow doe is picking her way through the birch and bluebells on the steep valley floor. She stops to look at me, brown eyes wide, ears and tail flicking. I take in her dark, mottled flank and the twitch of her muscles, the impulse to run rippling beneath her skin. I nod at James and point with my head towards the deer as she turns slowly, not hurrying, showing us the badger face of her black and white behind as she retreats up the valley side.

I feel slightly guilty that we're on a hostel campsite rather than at the side of the river. But being here is good. Running water, flushing toilets. I spoke to Jen earlier to say we were safe and well and said something similar to her, about how it's not possible to experience the thrill of an adventure when you're comfortable. A seasoned traveller, she gave me short shrift. But I remember a passage in Nancy Mitford's essay 'A Bad Time', which recounts Captain Scott's ill-fated push to the South Pole. She explains how the group often discussed whether they would 'continue to like Polar travel, if by aid of modern inter-ventions, it became quite easy and comfortable. They said no, with one accord. It seems as if they really wanted to prove to themselves how much they could endure. Their rewards were a deep spiritual satisfaction and relationships between men who had become more than brothers.'

James decides to turn in early but I sit by the fire to finish a miniature bottle of red wine I bought from the hostel's bar. The sap from the wood spits and cracks and I can hear the river below, tumbling over the rapids just after the campsite. I go and have a look but the water is almost invisible in the dark, just the black of the sky and the black of the water. No stars but the occasional white fizz of foam.

In the new light of day the valley seems changed. After travelling through a relatively low-lying landscape of soft, red sandstone and mudstone, where the river is free to wander and sprawl, we have now reached limestone. On the west bank, and possibly on the east further along, there are long stretches of hills dotted with lumps of grey rock that look like they have been tossed from their peaks. In the distance is a pointed crag, pines filling a cleft in the exposed rock face like a fuzz of chest hair. The river is wide and sweeping, shallow enough to expose gold-coloured stone beneath a surface that bubbles and dawdles.

A fisherman is standing on a beach by the corner. He shouts something and we get closer to see which way he wants us to go. He shouts again. He's got a 'fish on' and wants us to tell his friend downstream.

'You cannae miss him, he's in a red car. Tell him to come quick.' He seems terrified, as if he never intended to catch anything; as if a quiet day by the river has been spoilt by the temerity of a greedy fish. He gets out his mobile as we move past, presumably to his friend, realising that modern communications might be quicker than canoe-mail. We wish him luck and keep going. A minute later a red car hammers past in a plume of dust on the east bank. The cavalry has arrived.

Getting closer to the crag, I see that the rock face is not smooth, but rather a woody hill where limestone projects over the river as it bends away to the west. The rocks are hung with garlands of shrub and snaggling tree roots; chipped and lined with black gullies; stained with leaching minerals and dripping water. They look like the prows of three giant ships, or perhaps faces. Heavy-browed Easter Island heads, weatherworn and battered, staring out over meadows and towards the hills we've left behind. These are Coldwell Rocks, one of the favourite subjects of the Romantics who came here to draw and paint, making postcards of a captured landscape.

At the start of the meander, directly under Coldwell Rocks and opposite the yellow-sand beach that has formed along the inside of the curve, large lumps of limestone have fallen to create a canoe-sized harbour. We nudge the Pipe inside and stretch out on flat slabs of rock, already warmed by the sun; basking like seals before rolling off to cool down and float in the water.

Our little rock port is full of young fish. As we lie still they come to investigate us, nosing at our feet and legs. I don't move and watch one darting through my legs, wriggling away with body-wobbling speed at a sign of movement. I open my hand and place it underneath a fish the size of my middle finger. I expect it to move but it remains there as I close my hand round it and bring it to the surface. It's a young dace, its flank shimmering silver, with a flash of yellow along its belly, its mouth opening and closing out of the water. I show James, who asks if he should call the man in a red car, and lower the fish back in the water, opening my fingers and feeling it wriggling through.

As we reach the village of Symonds Yat, the water is still full of other canoes and kayaks. Hire boats make their way upstream, away from the rapids, while growing bands of kayakers gather on concrete slipways – a luminous mess of neoprene, bright helmets and flapping spray decks – readying themselves for the white water round the next bend.

The rapids are classed as Grade-2, defined as a continuous rapid with waves, small stoppers, obstructions and the possibility of strong eddies and cushion waves (the cushion of water that builds up on the upstream of a rock). There is said to be an obvious route through, a chute, but as it will be our first taste of proper white water we decide to play it safe and walk the bank to check it out. The air is misted with spray from the torrent below, a perpetual drizzle that forms rainbow bursts over the whole wooded gorge.

Although the gradient of the bedrock is natural, for the last two centuries it has been subjected to various engineering works. The island the river surges round was formed from the dumped slag of Symonds Yat's iron ore mines. To the right of the island are shallow rapids, and to the left a wider, deeper cascade: a rolling boil of green water. On both sides the water gains speed over a step, the current forming into a white-headed arrow.

The canoeists and kayakers are all heading for the route to the left of the island, closest to the steep, rocky east bank. The water hits off the first line of rocks, crashing back into the oncoming current to form a continuous peaked wave, foaming and teetering, forever threatening to break. A second line of rocks cuts out from the left, creating sucking troughs and more waves that slop and spill against the flow. If the sight of the river wasn't enough, the sound is tremendous: a flat, hollow roar. It's like standing on the hard shoulder of a motorway. Even the curmudgeonly Gilpin was impressed, stating that 'the violence of the stream, and the roaring of the waters, impressed a new character' on the solemnity and majesty of the valley. 'All was agitation, and uproar and every steep, and every rock stared with wildness, and terror.'

For the past 200 years these rapids have been used for pleasure, for thrills. From the late 1800s rowing boats carrying six to twelve people navigated the gorge. Since the 1950s canoeists and kayakers have adopted this place – a training ground for Olympic competitors and International Expedition canoeists. But the rapids, a draw for those on foot as much as those on water, were very nearly lost. In 1996 the previous landowners considered dredging them to make them more suitable for fishing. A crisis meeting was held: senior paddlers and representatives from British Canoeing and Canoe Wales came together to form the Symonds Yat Rapids Preservation Group. Through a national appeal and support from various organisations including the Environment Agency, the purchase of the rapids was announced in 2003.

We walk back to the canoe, edging along paths full of people with their eyes on the river. The kayakers on the water are all wearing protective headgear. While we haven't got white-water helmets, we do have cycle helmets. We strap them on at the last possible moment, feeling slightly ridiculous. I'm glad my wife can't see me. I used to rib her mercilessly for wearing a velvet riding hat while she cycled around Brighton; an equestrian eventer with a metal steed.

We bide our time and ease out into the river, deciding to take the middle channel. It looks like the calmest route, the point at which we are furthest away from the rocks and the raging water. James is almost beside himself with excitement. He is a natural thrill-seeker. An adrenaline junkie who rides mountain bikes up and down almost vertical slopes, who would think nothing of giant jumps and the possibility of falling. But I am nervous.

Before we left a friend had told me how his son had capsized coming through Symonds Yat, badly cutting his leg on rocks. I keep thinking about what would happen if I fell out: the idea of the water turning red; of breaking bone; of having to be rescued. I'm probably just as concerned about losing face in front of so many other paddlers. I try and push the thought from my mind. It's too late to hesitate now anyway, after just a few strokes the current has us. There's no turning back. The water swells behind us, pushing us to the point where the river humps over a step of rock into the rapids.

The noise is unreal, a thousand washing machines on full spin; the spray wets our faces. We're paddling fast, both out of nervousness but also determined to hit the right spot, not to be pulled to the right or the left. We pause as the nose of the Pipe reaches the step, the canoe rising slightly with the water before sliding in.

What is only seconds feels like hours, a freeze-frame sequence where every heartbeat, every movement of the hips and legs and paddle stroke can almost be calmly observed before time whooshes back onto the river, rushes into the ears with the water's roar. The Pipe's bow dips, goes under the water, before bouncing up and clear.

We holler, involuntary shouts – not joy, not fear, but something wilder – paddling hard to hold course and keep away from the rocks on the right. There's no time to relax or think. We're now fighting the river to keep off the rocks on the other side; leaning, shifting our weight. It feels like we are going over as we steer against the current. The power of the water is immense. It is a sensation of liquid muscles that flex and pull, ripple and bulge.

The canoe stays upright and squirts through the chute onto water that whirls and spits but no longer looks likely to smash us against rocks. I can see people now. A group of kayakers sit at the end of the island, each holding onto the other's craft while they converse in shouts over the roar of the water. One raises his paddle at us and we wave back. There is no slowing down in this current, so instead we rudder again, aiming for a scallop-shaped beach on the south bank.

My hands are shaking. I'm buzzing. I thought the adrenaline rush would be different. Clean. But instead it reminds me of that slightly giddy feeling I would get as a child after nearly falling off my bike when flying round a corner or hitting a kerb.

A close scrape. It is the danger that makes the difference. It amplifies the senses and experience: sometimes so that each moment becomes crystal-clear and perfect, while at other times the self is almost completely overwhelmed. It is a wave that crashes against you, pulling back to leave a dry mouth and blood pumping. Mortality exposed and, in the same instant, life affirmed. I don't quite know what to make of it. Did I enjoy it? I think I did. Do I want more? I'm not sure.

For some it is a desire for these kinds of experiences that brings them to rivers like the Wye and motivates them to seek out even wilder waters. After all, here at Symonds Yat the rapids are only rated as Grade 2 out of a possible 6. It's difficult to imagine what the higher grades would be like: the severe waves, drops and stoppers of Grade 4 in places like the River Erme and the Tees; the long, violent rapids of Grade 5 found dashing from mountains (Ogwen in Snowdonia, Nevis in Scotland and the gorge section of the River Coe), their congested routes making even rescue difficult. As for Grade 6, its basic definition is 'not runnable'. A mission impossible. I've only ever seen pictures online. Boiling waters that churn and crash over boulders, ragged rocks and down sizeable falls. On one, an image of a Scottish river in spate, the head of a kayaker can just be seen at the top of the run, his yellow helmet a beacon against the bone-white froth. The caption says he ended the day in hospital.

On land we strip out of drysuits and sit with our feet in the water. The foreshore is littered with iron ore, big chunks that resemble meteorite shards. The nodules look like fat worm casts, the surface bubbled and waved from iron meeting oxygen. I put a couple in my kit bag and lie back, scanning the skies for a sign of peregrines. I've heard they nest in the crags at Coldwell Rocks and I'm hoping to glimpse one. A pigeon attempts a passable impression but it's the closest I get.

On the water, some of the kayakers we passed on the way down are attempting an ascent, heads down, paddles whirring. One makes it, his hips twitching and edging the kayak at almost impossible angles. The other two hang in the water, moving neither forward nor backward: a war of attrition they can't possibly win. Eventually they turn, edging their kayaks into a calm spot of water between rocks while their friend enjoys the spoils of victory – a heart-quickening helter-skelter down the left side, his head almost disappearing in the white foam that leaps from the rocks. A man in an open canoe is also on the way back up, using a pole to inch himself over the rocks. It looks exhausting. I'm glad we haven't got one.

James's voice floats over my shoulder.

'Oh man, I'd love to try that.'

'Yeah, me too,' I lie, 'me too.'

We run the rapids three more times, stowing our gear behind trees, and floating the Pipe upstream through the shallows by the east bank. The walk is hard going, the river bed scoured and uneven, the white water obscuring sight of the pits and rolling stones on the bottom. But the ride down is worth it.

First we repeat the middle route, before becoming braver and riding the cushioned wave to the right, ruddering desperately against the sucking swell from the rocks. It's fun but it's not like it was before. Tamed by repetition, the edge and intensity of the thrill has gone; the sense of fear that gave the experience its complex high notes. I need a bigger, wilder hit. Perhaps I could get hooked on white water after all.

It takes longer than it should to reach Monmouth. The adrenaline that had boosted our heart rates and expanded our lungs is starting to leave our bodies. I feel tired, drained, like someone has put kryptonite under my seat. James says he feels the same, as if he left something very important back at the rapids. We try to kick-start our systems by taking it in turns to tumble out of the canoe. Lying on our backs, we drift downstream, not so much swimming as floating, feeling the water pull us round like leaves. I test myself, seeing how far I dare to go from the canoe before flipping onto my front and trying to stand against the flow. The water is strong, stubborn, not willing to release; it has suddenly become aware of my presence. The Wye is the hungry, deceitful stream again.

We both talk constantly about the river: its beauty; the speed of its flow; its rapids. Before now, I always thought those who hunted for white water were more concerned about conquering it – about showing that technique and technology can beat the elements, that human skill can overcome whatever nature throws at it. Or maybe I thought they were interested in the thrill, but not so much in the environment that helped generate it. But I think I was wrong. Of course there is a thrill at being good at something, but there is a reason why people look for rivers like these away from the artificial runs of white-water centres. The jeopardy, the necessary threat of the water, brings with it a greater connection to place and intensifies the appreciation of the environment. The risk helps peel away the distance. Flesh and bone are given up to the water, the pump of a quickened heart matches the river's flow. The body can feel the power of the river, through it, round it.

The term 'thrill seeker' for white-water enthusiasts is too dismissive, too glib. They are, when it comes down to it, river seekers.

CHAPTER 8

Alone on the water

I t feels strange to be heading towards a river on my own. Snowed under with work, James has stayed at home, meaning that this will be my first solo trip. It's an opportunity, though, to experience a river alone, to see if that sense of waterborne freedom grows in solitude or fades without comradeship. I do feel nervous. I have never actually paddled a canoe by myself and I know that technique, so readily abandoned in previous trips, will play a big part here.

Last night I sat on my hotel bed with a paddle, examining and testing my J stroke (a way to push forward and easily correct the course of the canoe) against YouTube videos; racing rapids with grizzled Canadian outdoorsmen while sat with a duvet over my knees. Not only am I without James, I'm also without the Pipe. Too heavy for me to handle alone, I've bought a 16-foot canoe at mate's rates from a friend. Estuary-green, the Pipette is already lined and furrowed from adventures on previous rivers and I'm keen to add my own.

The West Country is full of rivers; sogging and jogging down from hill and moor. On the drive from Suffolk the road shuttled me over the Tone, the Axe, the Exe and the romantically named King's Sedgemoor Drain – a channel that diverts the Cary and discharges into the Parrett. Canoeists I have spoken to all have recommendations about where to paddle: the Dart; the Exe; the Tamar; the Taw and Torridge, following Tarka's mythical swim. But it is the River Otter I'm drawn to.

Rising in the Blackdown Hills, near Otterford in Somerset, it flows for just 20 miles through east Devon before reaching the Channel to the west of Lyme Bay on the Jurassic Coast. I've heard that the Otter, by no means big, its name alone evocative of watery wildness, is a place of quiet beauty. What's more, it is also home to a wild population of beavers and after paddling through landscapes where they once would have roamed – their bones have been found in the caves of the Wye Valley – the idea of being alone on the water with these creatures is utterly bewitching.

I'd been shown on a map where the beavers had last been seen on the Otter, two loose pencil-drawn circles on the upper and lower sections of the river. Targets to be hit. Ideally I would put in by the estuary's mouth at Budleigh Salterton and make my way inland with the tidal rush, but time is not on my side. According to my reckoning the sea will be retreating – not to return until the early hours – by the time I arrive. I'm also slightly concerned that I will be unable to move in the current; a greenhorn in a green canoe. Instead I decide to follow winding roads towards Otterton, where I park overlooking the river at the village's red-brick mill.

Getting the canoe down is a back-breaking, slapstick routine. I inch it from the roof rack, getting my head and shoulders under the wooden yoke, gradually taking more and more of the canoe's weight until I'm staggering round the car park with a 16-foot hat, see-sawing towards the ground.

The cloud has been thick all day, the sky the colour of bleached bone. But now the sun is beginning to break through, dancing over clear water and down to a stone bed the colour of lightly baked biscuit. To the right is the road bridge, made of sand-coloured ashlar, its triple arches sweeping down into pointed cutwaters. The water upstream of the bridge dips over stone and rushes through, the flow forming a pebbled bar in front of the bridge's central pier. The bank by the mill is steep and grassy, contoured by a muddy, twisting track made by dogs as they gallop and scramble in and out of the water.

I walk the Pipette out into the river, the water pushing and coursing but little more than ankle-deep. I get in and position myself, kneeling into the side of the canoe to 'heel' her, making it easier to reach the water but also shortening the waterline and giving me greater control.

With my weight inside, the bottom of the canoe is touching the bed, but she's not grounded. I feel the ripple of stone travel through the boat and into my knees as I ease her forward, away from the shallows of the bridge and towards the east bank, ducking under a horse chestnut with cream-and-raspberry-ripple candles of blossom. The lower branches drag in the water, their leaves like flattened fingers; like beaver tails. I knew lack of water might be a problem, and although there is enough to carry the boat it is hard to complete a full stroke, the paddle bounces off the bed, the wood ringing flat against stone. I try and stay with the current, where a deeper route has been scoured into the bed.

On the west bank, dog walkers and joggers are making the most of the change in the weather. The bank screens everything from below the chest, making it look as if they too are floating. Swishing Gore-Tex apparitions. To the east the river is fringed with clumps of wet woodland, melancholy tresses of willow and late-to-leaf alder, giving way to thickets of dense scrub packed with wild garlic, whose scent lies heavy in the valley. The flowers are pure white against Hulk-ish green. Behind the trees I can occasionally see a cliff of red sandstone, its face pocked and pecked by wind and rain to create gurning masks that stare out over the river.

I move slowly, letting the sensation of being alone wash over me; a sense of freedom to wander; feeling the river completely, every movement of it mine. It is startling how different paddling solo is. From the first trip to now, it felt like the act of setting out on water was crossing a boundary. Breaking the surface was to connect with the river's flow and become, in some way, part of it. But now that sensation is intensified. My movements themselves, my arms and hands, my whole body, are liquid and full of current. I spend whole minutes just drifting, sighing with a 'this is the life' contentment – combined with deep relief that I'm actually managing to move forward.

The river is full of beaches, crying out to be lounged on, but I'm not ready to stop. Opposite me the red rock is completely exposed and the unshielded surface has been worked by the wind and rain to reveal flat stones that jut out like jagged steps. Stepping stones to the centre of the earth. They remind me of the armoured back-plates of a stegosaurus. Lighter colours cut through the red rock; orange fading to whey-ish yellow. Two willows teeter on the cliff edge, roots gripping the vertical rock face beneath them, exploring the fissures and cracks, like the tentacles of an octopus hunting for fish in a reef.

The path behind me is still busy. This is a popular walking route, both for locals and for tourists who walk from the sea up to the tea rooms of the mill, retracing a route Samuel Taylor Coleridge probably took when he grew up around here. Many of them want to talk, and there is only one topic of conversation: beavers.

Before I embarked on my solo voyage, I met up with wetland ecologist Mark Elliott to see a beaver project currently being run by Devon Wildlife Trust in the headwaters of the Tamar. At a secret location in the west of the county, beavers have been introduced into a 7-acre enclosure to see if their felling, damming and browsing will help restore the wet, heathy, grazing pasture of important Culm Grassland that has been encroached by scrub.

It wasn't hard to see the impact the beavers have made in the six years since they were released. Just a few feet from the solar-powered electric fence that contains them, a tree had been nibbled all the way round, almost to its heart; the whole weight of the trunk resting on a slender column of white wood. Perfectly symmetrical, it could have been turned on a lathe. But the marks from chisel-like incisors that bit into this tree are clear to see; rasping across the grain, an instinctive attempt by an animal to bend the landscape to its will. The tree is the tip of the iceberg. Since 2011 the beavers have successfully restored the grassland; turning woody thickets into glades rich with all kinds of wildlife.

Not far from the gnawed tree was one of the site's thirteen dams that have helped bring about such dramatic change. Before my visit I supposed beavers felled trees to make dams; I visualised them as grand log cabins rising high out of the water. But although beavers can take out sizeable trees, they only do so to graze. They don't eat the wood, but the young bark of willow shoots. This first dam was small and low, almost unnoticeable; made from sticks, roots and earth. For beavers, the main purpose of dams is to create standing water of a depth of at least two feet near their burrow, allowing them to come and go without surfacing. But as well as giving them safety, dams are also seedbanks: tiny beaver allotments. The gnawed willow will come again and be grazed from the water.

The dams in the enclosure hold up to one million tonnes of additional water. In six years, the surface water on the site has increased from 108 square yards to 2,150, with the largest pond holding nearly 50,000 gallons. What was once a small stream that drained four arable fields is now a complex wetland system of ponds and canals.

The results of research at this site have been nothing short of extraordinary, providing clear evidence that beavers can have a significant effect on the reduction of flooding downstream, even during prolonged wet periods, such as when Storm Frank lashed the country in December 2015, causing rivers to burst their banks, flooding roads and homes. Here, on average, peak flows during storm events were 30 per cent lower leaving the site than entering. It seems clear that having beavers on our waterways that feed into rivers could clearly bring major benefits.

But it's not just flood waters that beavers manage; they can combat drought too. The dams, despite the best efforts of their creators, are leaky, slowly releasing a steady trickle of stored water. It means that long after the rain has stopped, the flow of water off the site continues. When a month of sunshine in the summer of 2016 left the incoming channel and the top two beaver ponds bone-dry, base flow from the enclosure continued. The low water levels, with the associated problems of depleted oxygen and high concentrations of pollutants, simply did not materialise.

The mud-topped dams that regulate the movement and storage of water also clean it. Storm water leaving the enclosure was found to contain three times less sediment than when it arrived, while pollutants such as nitrates and phosphates were also significantly reduced. Meanwhile dissolved organic carbon, often severely depleted in intensively managed grasslands, was found to have been restored by the carbon-rich environment of a fully functioning wetland.

Wildlife has been quick to respond. Counts of frogspawn have gone up from ten clumps in 2011 to 681 in 2017. Aquatic invertebrates have also increased, responding almost immediately to the habitat changes: in the first year of the project the number of species went up from fourteen to forty-one. As invertebrates thrived, other species have moved in: less common bats, such as natterer's and barbastelle; kingfishers, heron, willow tits, grass snakes.

I found the beaver's lodge, a huge compost-heap-sized bundle of sticks that humps out of a large, deep pond, surrounded by floating sweet grass and a few ungnawed trees, at the bottom of the enclosure. Looking back, with the fences again out of view, there was a real sense of wildness. That small sloping piece of land, now terraced with dams, trickling and oozing with water, felt almost primeval. It was a glimpse of a lost landscape that could just be about to return.

Over the last few decades, the beaver has already been reintroduced into many other countries in Europe, including those with dense populations such as the Netherlands. In 2016, 400 years after being hunted to extinction for their fur, flesh and castoreum (a beaver secretion used in everything from pain-killers to perfume), the Scottish government announced that the Eurasian beaver was to be formally recognised as a native species, which meant that populations in both the Knapdale Forest and on the River Tay would be allowed to remain.

Beavers were probably first seen here on the River Otter in 2007, but remained a well-kept secret for many years. As the water in the river was deep enough to make damming on the main flow unnecessary, they weren't really having a vis-ible impact. It was only when the beavers began breeding and a camera-trap image of kits went public in 2014 that Defra intervened. The government proposed removing them, but fol-lowing a fierce local campaign, Devon Wildlife Trust proposed a five-year monitoring trial in partnership with the University of Exeter, the Derek Gow Consultancy and Clinton Devon Estates. Their bid, backed up by their experience with the pro-ject in the enclosure, was accepted. The beavers, part of two family groups of nine beavers on the Otter, were given a health check and re-released in March 2015. There are now thought to be twenty-seven beavers living on the river in different family groups between Honiton and the river's estuary at Budleigh Salterton.

The beavers' future on the river is as uncertain as how they first got there. The River Otter trial ends in 2020, and despite the support of both landowners and public (Devon Wildlife Trust raised £500,000 towards the trial through crowdfunding) and government commitments in 2017 to more enclosed schemes in the Forest of Dean, there is the possibility that the animals could be removed. It is a depressing thought. For me, it was also an added incentive to get on the river.

The sense of excitement and enthusiasm about this river is amazing. The beavers have had an impact much greater than their effect on the landscape: they have won people's hearts, and in so doing have put the health of the river back on the agenda. A fascination with beavers, their habits and movements, has led naturally to a greater understanding of the whole ecosystem.

A woman with tight curly hair, clinging to a freshly trimmed poodle called Coco, has been hoping to see them for months. 'Everyone is really pleased to have them,' she says. 'I think there is a sense of protectiveness about them too. It just feels like they should be here.' A few minutes later a man walking a panting chocolate Labrador says he was lucky enough to see a young kit: 'It came towards me and almost stood up in the water. But it was off like a rocket as soon as I tried to take a photograph,' he smiles at the memory. 'It really was the most beautiful little thing.' A group of three women, clad in lycra, take a breather from a run to ask if I've seen a beaver. They say they are heading upstream where they've been told there's a better chance of spotting one.

Further downstream a stone beach pushes out into the river. The current scours a narrow path under a fallen willow, but I think I can get through. The clarity of the water gives an illusion of shallowness and I step out, only to sink up to my neck. The water sings around me and forces the air out of my lungs in a high-pitched 'Oh'. Although it's not serious, it's a small reminder that I'm on my own; that I shouldn't be too confident or careless. There is no one to pull me out, or to raise an alarm. The water, for all of my grand feelings of holistic union, would take my bones.

Despite my surprise I have managed to keep hold of the canoe's rear painter, and with a fair amount of splashing manage to push the willow's branches to one side, allowing the Pipette to squeak back into open water. I move alongside her and, with a hand on each side, flop myself in. Now free to move, the canoe skips away while I reach for the paddle, dipping her nose over a stony drop and sliding onto part of the river that is deep and still, the current falling away as if suddenly tired of the rush.

There are no dams on this part of the Otter. The water downstream is deep enough already. Beavers may be engineers, but only if it is required. Given the choice they would go for a turn-key property rather than a renovation job. The signs of their presence are more subtle, less likely to be picked up by someone who isn't really looking for them. The animals that have caused such a fuss here could be all around us.

There are rumours of beavers on the Thames and the Severn in Gloucester, while Mark Elliott said earlier that there are certainly beavers in Kent and on the Tamar. I slow the canoe. Along the east bank I spot a couple of willows that have also toppled into the water. But on these I can clearly see that the branches have been chewed, nibbled off to leave six-inch stakes of heart-piercing sharpness. Two other trees have been grazed, with new growth already coming through – nature's coppice, a cut-and come-again salad bar for beavers. I glide closer. In the water are a few thin branches, stripped of bark, just like some of the sticks I saw at the enclosure. I feel a rush of excitement. I must be in one of the pencilled circles.

I paddle further downstream, hugging the bank to look for more signs but, seeing none, I turn slowly round, heading beyond the first beaver-coppiced willow where I had noticed the bank shelves slightly. I float beneath the overhang of an old alder and wait for a few walkers to go by before scrambling up onto the bank, breathing hard as I heave the Pipette behind me. I hide her in some bushes and set off to explore.

The wood runs back some 40 feet. It's not as dense as I thought; a mix of young willow and sycamore, the ground carpeted in wild garlic, whose smell grows stronger as it bruises under my boots. The trees thin out to bramble in front of a sandstone cliff, its higher reaches glowing in the sun. A sparrowhawk takes off from a nearby tree, drops like she has been shot, before rising back into view, the feathers on her light-brown back looking almost scaled as she arrows through the branches.

Setting up camp alone feels slightly strange, but at least the routine is soothingly familiar: pacing the gap between the trees and resting the hammock on my shoulders as I reach round the sycamore for the other ends; tying the bow as high as I can. I return to the canoe and drag it over to the camp, the smell of wild garlic filling the air again. Although there has been no rain recently, the ground is still damp and the Pipette will be somewhere to sit and eat tonight, somewhere to write. I can hear the occasional voice from across the river but I still feel hidden, comfortably out of sight.

It's only when I'm making tea and hear the repetitive knocking-tap of a walking stick that I realise my camp is not as secluded as I thought. Another path cuts across the top of the wood-fringed cliff. High above me a walker is looking down at me. I don't know what to do. I suddenly feel horribly exposed.

I try to appear nonchalant, but I imagine that with my hoody up and snood pulled to my nose, I come across as dodgy. After unlocking eyes I stare out at the water, waiting for the man to call out to me, to demand that I get off his land. I retreat instead into my hammock. The joy of being settled and comfortable has been replaced with anxiety, a fear of being moved on. It is a stupid sensation. I reason with myself that it doesn't matter if I am asked to leave. It would be a pain in the arse to pack up again, but really, who cares? It would have been so different if James was here. Safety even in small numbers. He probably would have made friends, invited him down for a drink.

I try to relax again and listen to the buzz-rolling drum of a woodpecker hammering into a tree nearby and the throaty, milk-bottle-blow coos of pigeons. Each call an unanswered question. *Who whooo who who? Woo hooo hoo hoo?* From my hammock I can't see the movement of the river, but the bank has its own flow. Cleavers, hogweed and ground-creeping ivy. A wave of greens, frothed with the spittle-white flowers of garlic.

I keep looking at my watch, willing the minutes and hours to pass and the sun to dim. I'm still nervous about being seen. The walkers keep coming, making their way along a trail from Budleigh Salterton up to Otterton. Only one spots me on the opposite bank, the blue of the tarp being lighter than the darkening wood. I hear them surmise that it must be a beaver-spotter. By half-eight, though, the river is mine alone. I sit on a stump and watch the water while drinking tea. The surface is smooth, the smoothest I've seen all day, no longer pushed by wind or ruffled by duck feet.

I've gone to my hammock for my notepad when I hear a gentle splash, and turn to see what looks like the end of an otter's tail. Bubbles spin out from the widening circles and track towards the darkness of the west bank. The river collects itself, the water calming and coming together. I strain to locate where I had found the freshly gnawed willow, but it's just out of sight. It's tempting to go and investigate, but I know from months watching foxes on a patch of land near my house that to move is to miss out. I try and make myself comfortable again, drawing up my snood and pulling down the front of my hood against the clouds of gnats that have started to gather, trying to ignore them as they settle and chew on my wrists and ankles.

It's about half an hour later when I hear a noise, a bigger splash than before. I strain through the darkness again. The water remains unbroken, just a few ripples arcing out from the same trees I had sheltered beneath earlier on. And then, out of the gloom, a beaver.

I can't believe how sleek it is. In the same way that I was surprised when I first saw a badger running at speed – its fur rippling like cuttlefish frills – I am taken aback by how beautiful, graceful and serene this beaver is. I had expected it to blunder and crash, but it glides, cutting through the water in silence. It's travelling upstream, away from its chewed coppice and under willow that hangs out over the east bank, straining the water. I follow it with my eyes, my hands gripping the edges of the stump almost to hold me down – to prevent myself from chasing after it, calling out to it in pure, stupid joy. I whisper to myself again and again: 'It's a bloody beaver.'

I wait for five minutes before I dare to move; the river now feels like it's bursting with crepuscular life, those animals that live for the magical spaces between day and night. I head for a clear treeless section and sit, my toes almost brushing the surface of the water. On the opposite bank I think I see a movement, my brain filling in the gaps my eyes cannot see. I can make out something, three patches of not-so-dark. A surface that reflects back the little light there is, three dull moons. I only realise they are faces when I see one of them lowering binoculars. They must be here for the beavers too. I don't know if they've seen me, but my instinct is to retreat again. I don't want to break my peace any more than they probably want me to break theirs.

I creep back to camp and fire up the stove and text James to tell him about the sighting. I know he'll be gutted to have missed it and I feel a sadness at not being able to share it. A pair of tawny owls calls in the darkness. The female *ke-wick* answered by the indignant jowly wobble, *hooooo-hooooo*. Her calls come faster and faster. I scan the sky but it's violet, black, dense, brushed felt, the night thickened and given depth by the trees and the looming shadow of the cliff. Faster and faster the calls come; louder. She's travelling past, 20 feet, maybe less, the male's voice almost breaking in excited anticipation at her arrival, the restrained *hoooo-hooooo* becoming a panted *hoo-hoo-hoo-hoo-hoo-hoo*. A last *ke-wick*. As defined and sharp as a twig snap. Silence returns as talons grip and wing feathers settle. I imagine the pair of them huddled together in the dark, their duet over. The water takes over from the air, splinking, tinkling, spluttering on. My phone vibrates. It's James. 'If you didn't get a picture, it didn't happen.'

I had been worried about doing this trip without James. The danger didn't bother me. Still foolhardy. I was confident about being on the water but I was worried about being alone. In fact, I can't remember the last time I have been totally by myself for more than a couple of hours. I haven't really had time to think about it too much while I've been paddling today, too focused on keeping the canoe going forward and looking out for signs of beavers, the river working me, flowing round and into me, probing and peeling back the layers. But now, with time to think, I can't help but wonder if these trips have been an escape for me, about running away from it all: responsibilities, stress, expectations. Was the nostalgic pang I felt for lost child-hood freedoms on the Colne about flight? Less about memory and more about a waterborne retreat from adult life?

But no. These journeys have not been about escaping life, but making it. Each trip has been an experience. I think they have been a test too, about – and I feel stupid even forming the words – proving myself a man. Capable, useful, fit.

When I was a child I used to think about war a lot, spending hours talking to my grandfather about what he'd seen and heard as he pushed across Europe with Allied troops. His half-track exploding; the sniper's bullets stripping bark from the tree where he was hiding. I used to, and occasionally still do, wonder how I would have coped, how I would have reacted. Would I have survived as both of my grandfathers did? Or would it have been the end of a family line in a shell-blasted field?

Perhaps it's pointless macho stuff, but exploration, as hackneyed as it sounds, is related to self-discovery and it is often born from closeness to death: from the terrifying beauty of ice, the breathless cold of mountains. I tell myself off again. Canoeing in the West Country is hardly dealing with crushing ice flows and crevasses. I am not Richard Byrd, isolated and alone, fending off the madness of six months of Antarctic solitude. But I am learning things about myself. Sitting here now, alone, I'm surprised at just how happy I feel. Soothed and calmed by the water and the peace that darkness brings.

I pull the hood of my sleeping bag up over my head and lie with my face pointing towards the gap in the tarp, the swinging movement of the hammock slowing to a heartbeat swish. There are the usual night sounds, the ground is alive with tiny creatures. A scuttering rush through rat runs and vole holes. It feels as if even worms make a sound as they move through the earth, a rustling, swallowing pop. Something large is making its way through the scrub, browsing as it goes. I can hear the pull and then the whipping-back of branches. A deer? I peer out into the darkness, hoping to see a shape or a movement in the gloom.

I had hardly slept the previous night. The walls of the hotel were paper-thin, the noise of other people's TVs bubbling through to join the low, window-rattling hum of the M5. Conversations, flushed toilets and the flat slam of heavy doors. The sounds out here are a gentle, soothing relief in comparison.

I drift off, only to come to again with a hypnic jerk. My response to the muscle twitch sets the hammock swinging again, rustling over a branch I couldn't bring myself to remove. Then I hear something else. A crack. A chanking chew. It is the gnaw of a beaver, its teeth nibbling and flaying the willow stands. I'm tempted to get up and try and catch a glimpse, but both the noise I make getting out and the beam of my torch will surely disturb it. Anyway, I'm too tired to move. I sink back down in my sleeping bag, happy just to listen, happy that it's there at all. A tiny splinter of wild.

Getting out of the hammock in the morning is always hard. It is an amniotic sac, with the watery heartbeat of the river fluttering away outside. I poke my head out. It's dry. No rain overnight and even the dew is light. The sun is yet to reach the valley, and although the birds have been singing for hours, the river and its banks are still relatively dark. I decide to make an early start and get back on the river before it gets busy. The sound of the gulls suggests the sea is not too far away and I like the idea of having my breakfast on the beach. I pack quickly and ease the canoe back onto the river, keeping hold of the painter as she jerks into the water like a fish on a line. I slip down the mud-bank on my backside and walk with the canoe until the water gets deeper, close to where I can see a new patch of willow has been whittled by beaver teeth.

The sky lightens slowly into a soft blue that fades out of and into a patchwork of high vapour-trail clouds. I pass under a bridge, where the first walkers of the day are crossing, look-ing down as I half-paddle and half-pole myself through, the depth of the water again not allowing a full stroke. The river is widening into an estuary and the land changes with it. The high, wooded banks give way to gentle beaches of mud, with the dull green of salt marsh behind. The wind is light. A cold breath. A *pirr* that makes a cat's paw on the water.

Following the meander is one of the most contented experi-ences of my life. It is deliriously beautiful. Fish leap in front of me as I trail a swan through the deepest channels, getting out once or twice when even she finds herself grounded. Herring gulls too make use of the shallows, their grey and white plum-age looking hand-painted and perfect. They take flight in shouting gangs as I get close. I'm not sure of the tide times but there is hardly any current at all, even when another tributary joins the main flow. On the east bank is a stand of straggling

Scots pines, bare from the trunk. The wind must rush through here, stunting everything but the topmost branches. They look positively Jurassic. The red sandstone rock they cling to sweeps down to a jutting headland, blanketed in grass and heathery scrub, while from the west a shingle spit, in places 20 feet high, rushes to meet it.

The river picks its way forward, plotting a course through the landscape. As it swings parallel to the spit the water deepens and curves back round towards the sea. The red of the rock fades from bright ochre to a spilt-milk white, a velvet cake of mud and rock, the layers delicate and defined. The base of the cliff is full of holes, the water burrowing in to create nooks and small caves. Great flat slabs of rock lie under them like dusty, freshly birthed icebergs, sand-coloured and smooth. The cliff's slow retreat inland can be traced by a snail-trail of older rocks, now green with algae and crusted with sea life that stretches all the way to the shoreline.

I concentrate again on the water, the river now finally sprinting along the home straight, eager to reach the sea. I paddle hard, shooting over a stone step on an icy jet, the current carrying me out to the bay. There is part of me that just wants to keep going for ever. To never stop. I feel hugely free. In fact I'm not sure I could stop right now even if I tried. I stop paddling, just moving my body to slalom the canoe along before she bursts out onto the sea, the tension going out of the water with a gulping slap on the canoe's bow.

I let the Pipette wallow for a second and then steer her into the crescent-shaped bay at Budleigh Salterton, its houses huddled in a V-shaped pocket between the estuary and another red cliff. I strike out towards the town, hugging the coast but far enough out to avoid the breakers that hiss onto the shingle beach. I practise my strokes, enjoying the canoe's response to my paddle and the bounce put in her step by a gentle swell. In the distance I can see the hazy shimmer of Sandy Bay and, just beyond that, what must be Exmouth or Dawlish. I turn the Pipette round and dig deep to get back to the river mouth, only stopping when I can hear the stones growl underneath her.

The shingle is deep, clattering up over my shins as I drag the canoe out of the water. I set up the stove, putting on enough water for porridge and tea, and sit facing the sea. I can't stop smiling.

In terms of distance, I haven't come far or tackled tough water or braved torrid conditions, but for me this trip feels like a real achievement. Being out on my own has given me not only confidence but an increased sense of freedom. It is good to have company, to have someone to depend on, but I think I really needed to know – deep down at least – that I could depend on me.

I pick up my phone and put it down again. It's rare for a moment to be yours alone to enjoy.

CHAPTER 9

Shaped by the river

The river swings from the south-west towards the dark hump of the Wrekin. A ridge of volcanic rock, shrouded in trees, a radio mast pointing to the white sky, it dominates a landscape of water and sloping fields, lined with dense hedges and freckled with the fluffy pinpricks of sheep. From this thick snake of a meander, the River Severn bends south-east towards Leighton and the Ironbridge Gorge, where I hope to reach tonight.

The water is high. The willows that line both sides of the bank are no longer raking the surface but are half-submerged in flashing water the colour of molten milk chocolate. The weather may have been dry here, but upstream in the Black Mountains on the windswept slopes of Mount Plynlimon, where the Severn starts its long journey to the Bristol Channel, the rain has been heavy and consistent. It could be worse. The river has before, many times, claimed this whole valley, raiding fields, homes, businesses, leaving everything grimed and be-grotted, slimed and sludged. It is a reminder of the power of the water, its ability to shape and transform. To provide and destroy.

But rivers don't just shape the physical features of the land; they can help form the very identity of a region. Cities spring up around them; industries thrive and decline; the landscape responds to the river's flow.

I'm on my own again. Buoyed by my experience on the Otter, I want to test myself on a bigger river, somewhere I'll be able to really feel the power and difference of the water. The Severn. The second sister, Sabrina, sibling of Vaga, whose route of 220 miles through Shropshire, Worcestershire and Gloucestershire forms the longest river in the UK. It is a path that takes in cities and towns, the homes of man and industry, powered by a flow of 3,800 cubic feet per second – greater than any of the UK's other rivers.

I had first been drawn to the Severn by the idea of pad-dling the estuary; enticed by the thought of the raging bore; enchanted by Alice Oswald's poetry of the river at night, a place that seemed not quite of this world. But for once I listened to reason, to the warnings of strong currents and winds. The treacherous tide, the sucking mud. Now standing on the bank with the Riverside Inn at my back, I'm glad. I've found on the trips so far that there is a real sense of rivers being two distinct entities, non-tidal and tidal. Turning from bone-thin to fat with water, a thick, powerful estuarine sweep. But here, miles from the sea, this river already quivers and shakes with strength; it is a liquid limb that wraps round the land, linked inextricably with everything from its people and its language to its future and its past.

I get the last of my gear together and push the Pipette through a bank of nettles to the water's edge. This is the outside tip of the meander and the flow is fast. A few people from the beer garden are standing watching, pints in hand; ready for their afternoon entertainment. Ego outweighs trepidation. I don't want to look stupid. I step into the canoe, spreading my weight, and sink to my knees, positioning them both to the port side, heeling the boat and dipping the paddle into the water for the first time. Stroke, stroke. The wind hits the river's surface like thrown sand, speckling and rippling. Then the plates of water break, drifting apart to create a smooth channel through the disturbance, just big enough for a canoe. I enter the current, a white trail of bubbles like the lingering wake of a boat, a gulf stream that tears round bends and careers from side to side.

Past Leighton the river meanders again, this time more tightly, the current stronger, the wind now full of rain. On the drive down I noticed a lay-by overlooking this stretch. From the roadside it did look picturesque, a winding river framed by the neat green of grazed fields. A place for picnics in misted-up, rain-dampened cars and a stopping point for geography field trips. But on the river, there is no sense of this scale; its land-cutting power can't be framed and defined, only felt through the perspectives of steep, sun-baked mud cliffs, mined with sand martin burrows and licked with brown water. On the inside of the meander silt has built up. Otter prints zig-zag across it, a map of interest, a mustelid psychogeography of grass and rock. A sniff, a spraint and back to the water.

The rain is growing heavier now. It drums into the canoe, a maddening tip-tap that soaks through my woollen hat and sends water running down my face. Above the trees to the left is the square tower of a church, while to the right I can just see the pot-bellied curve of a power station's cooling towers, sandstone-pink against a hill that seems to cross the river.

Round the next bend there is another power station almost hidden in the trees on the right bank. Built centuries after the Industrial Revolution clanged into gear just downstream, this is the Art Deco building of the Ironbridge Power Station. Or, rather Ironbridge Power Station A, as it became known after a new facility was built further down to cope with the post-war demand for electricity. The two power stations operated in tandem for some twenty years until 1982, when the giant soot-black doors of Power Station A swung closed for the last time. It is a lovely building. A temple to the old gods of coal. The pattern of red and black tiles above the doors is still clear and the white paintwork that tops and tails the huge two-storey windows is crisp and bright.

There is an air of neglect, though, a sense that time, like the river, has moved on, taking the people and the communities that used to work here with it. Weeds spill from gutters and creep along window ledges. The steel walkway along its front is now an unkempt lawn of shin-tickling grass. Pipes and funnels that emerge above the banks are disappearing under the glacial creep of moss and weed.

I stop paddling to take shelter under a steel-truss road bridge that used to provide access to the power station. It too has been abandoned: both ends blocked, it is now a bridge to nowhere. Like the river, it has become a no man's land, dressed in barbed wire and pigeon shit. Greenery explodes from its sides. Ivy swings like vines, almost touching the water, shaking hands with the shoulder-high thickets of nettle that have sprouted from landlocked piers.

From here I can see signs on the power station: 'Danger', 'Keep Out'. I know if James was here he'd be pushing to go and have a look, to see exactly what was left behind when the power went out. There is something fascinating about these buildings, something I'd sensed back at the mills on the Colne. The remnants of a time when the river was so vital to the region's success. The end of that relationship, between people and the river, has left a vacuum on the banks. A brick shell that once contained a beating heart.

I can see the Iron Bridge from the slipway where I leave the canoe. In the nineteenth century, this wharf was one of the busiest places in the gorge: a clanking, creaking point of delivery and export. The grooves where the tracks that carried wagons to the river once ran still lead down to the water's edge.

The river runs through the heart of this place. Not just physically but through its history. The Severn both created the conditions for the Industrial Revolution and sustained it. When a lake formed by a wall of ice during the last Ice Age overtopped, a great torrent of water flowed through Gloucestershire, cutting through layers of coal, iron ore, clay and limestone, exposing the resources that would turn the Severn Gorge from a place of sleepy beauty into an industrial hub.

Although coal and limestone had been hacked from this valley since the Middle Ages, it was the arrival of Abraham Darby in 1709 that is credited with kick-starting the Industrial Revolution into smoking, stinking life and making this gorge one of the most important places in the world. The Darby name was to loom large in Coalbrookdale for generations. Seven decades after Abraham came to make the perfect cooking pot, it was his great-grandson who forged the bridge and effectively made the town's name.

The reasoning behind the Iron Bridge's construction was clear. The flow of the river could be temperamental, too fast in winter and too shallow in summer. But the iron structure, designed by Thomas Farnolls Pritchard and built at one of the most dramatic points on the gorge, was also a potent symbol of industrial power. The advertising campaign that immediately followed the bridge's construction continued for 100 years. Tourists who once flocked to the south coast, lured by the healing power of the salt water, were told that Ironbridge was the 'Brighton of the Midlands'. It was a place where they would not step into the water, but stride over it.

As with the Severn's sister, the Wye, writers and artists travelled from great distances to see the bridge. John Byng, Viscount Torrington wrote in 1784 that it must be 'one of the wonders of the world'. Not to be outdone, John Pinkerton added, in his *A General Collection of Best and Most Interesting Voyages and Travels in All Parts of the World* that the bridge was 'a stupendous specimen of the powers of mechanism'.

But not all of the artists were so upbeat. Some recognised the relationship between the river and the surrounding land: just as the river had influenced and impacted the fate and identity of those who lived and worked on its banks, it had also been shaped and changed by their actions. And, just as the Thames had been transformed from deity to tramp, progress would exact its price from the Severn.

In 1787, Charles Dibdin, a dramatist and songwriter, described how 'Coalbrookdale wants nothing but Cerberus to give you an idea of the heathen hell. The Severn may pass for the Styx'. The painting *Coalbrookdale by Night* by Philip de Loutherbourg, made some fourteen years later, illustrated

Dibdin's point. Focusing on the Bedlam Furnaces – a name itself that evokes a degree of mad fury – his painting shows the gorge and the Severn glowing red. The sky and water are ablaze.

The river, which was used to transport raw materials and finished iron, was said to be one of the busiest in Europe, second perhaps only to the Thames. By 1768, 400 vessels were trading between Gloucester and Welshpool, rising to 800 fifty years later. At least six ferry crossings were in operation within this stretch of the gorge, carrying materials and workers to forges, kilns and quarries. With the increase in population and the proximity to so much industry it's said the river smelt like an open sewer, wreathed in smoke from iron works, brick works and chain works and lit by the hellish, cracked-earth glow of the famous blast furnaces.

Then the most industrialised area in the world, the surrounding valley was pocked with limestone quarries; treeless strip mines; with countless holes, shafts and passages sunk into the hillside. The river itself, full of ships with oxblood sails, would have been framed by a ring of coal pits, ore pits and man-made mountains of shining black slag and spoil. The gorge even had its own tar tunnel. Originally intended as an underground canal, the workers cutting through the rock in 1787 struck bitumen. Its dark treacle flows added to the wealth and the stink of the gorge.

The river made this town, helped swell it from dirt tracks and a few scattered homes to a frontier for industry. But as progress continued its march, those industries gradually declined. The bridge was left behind, a focal point, spanning the river's banks and the ages of humanity. But even this monument to industry is at risk from the geology and river that created it.

The constant movement of the gorge's walls, which also causes local gardens to slip, has been slowly crushing the bridge, forcing the crown of its arch up by some four inches. The iron masterpiece, which cost around £6,000 when it was built, is now the subject of a £3.6 million crowdfunding appeal by English Heritage to restore it – the organisation's most expensive conservation scheme since it became an independent charity in 2015.

From the height of the bridge – and it is surprisingly high – the river looks calm and glossy, undisturbed by current or rain, perhaps creasing slightly as it disappears into the wooded valley upstream. I look the other way, seeing the trees reflected in muddy-coloured water. I spot my canoe upstream, a line of dark green on the grey slipway. Out of the shelter of the gorge the rain lashes into my face and blows down my hood. I can almost sense the river still testing the bridge's footings.

The gorge itself may be moving, as the river continues to cut into it, but the scars of its industrial past have healed. Looking at the lushness, the greenness of it all, it's hard to imagine what the place would have been like during its heyday in the 1790s, when this river of industry, of coal dust and tar, connected this gorge with the rest of the world.

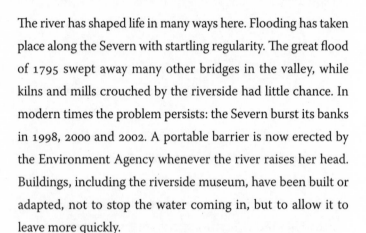

The river has shaped life in many ways here. Flooding has taken place along the Severn with startling regularity. The great flood of 1795 swept away many other bridges in the valley, while kilns and mills crouched by the riverside had little chance. In modern times the problem persists: the Severn burst its banks in 1998, 2000 and 2002. A portable barrier is now erected by the Environment Agency whenever the river raises her head. Buildings, including the riverside museum, have been built or adapted, not to stop the water coming in, but to allow it to leave more quickly.

I head back to the canoe to find a man standing over it, the flat-faced pug he's walking snuffling around its sides. He warns me about the rapids downstream. 'I've come out of there a couple of times in my canoe,' he says, looking at me with sad eyes from underneath a green cap, its peak blackened with rain. There's something about the way he talks that reminds me of *An American Werewolf in London*. It's a 'Stay on the road . . . beware of the moon' kind of warning, as if those huddled in Ironbridge's pubs and houses weren't sheltering from the rain but some other, more malign force.

The evening is drawing in but I don't feel ready to stop yet. I paddle along the river towards the bridge, the path I walked minutes before, slowly rising above me. The bridge was designed to be seen from the water, its side carrying the legend: 'This bridge was cast at Coalbrook-dale and erected in the year 1779.'

The Severn here is famous for its links to industry but it has also been, and still is, a river of leisure. The Ironbridge Rowing Club just upstream, which holds a regatta every year, was founded in 1870. And, despite its currents, the river has also been used for swimming. Captain Matthew Webb, the first person recorded to swim the English Channel, took his earliest strokes in the Severn. Webb, the son of a Coalbrookdale doctor, reportedly saved his own brother from drowning under the Iron Bridge. The Gorge Museum houses the silver chalice presented to Webb after the Channel crossing, along with a brandy flask bearing his initials. He was said to have taken warming draughts as he endured jellyfish stings and strong currents on a zig-zag course of 39 miles to Calais. The mighty Webb was finally defeated as he tried to swim the rapids at Niagara Falls in 1883; his body was recovered and buried in Oakwood Cemetery by the falls. A memorial erected at his birthplace at Dawley, near Telford, reads: 'Nothing great is easy!'

A floating swimming pool was also once built on the river here. Records of the plans suggest it was 50 feet long and 16 feet wide, with a wooden floor sloping from 2 feet 6 inches to 5 feet deep and folding doors to connect it to the river. Seventy-two barrels kept it and its changing rooms afloat. It opened in 1789 with a weekly average of more than 300 people making use of it in the summer of 1880. But the pool was short-lived. The tempestuous river washed it away the following winter.

Fishing has long been popular here too. The Ironbridge Angling Society describes itself as one of the oldest in Britain, with links back to the days of the Cope-Darby families and the land they owned along the banks of the Severn. Coracles – small, rounded, lightweight boats, often used for fishing – were once ubiquitous on the river; nearly every home had one. They would hang them from trees when not in use, the bowl-shaped craft looking like bizarre turtle roosts of wood and hide. One family, the Rogerses, was famous for making coracles, fashioning the craft in the shadow of the Iron Bridge for generations. The last descendant, Eustace Rogers, died in 2003. It doesn't seem a stretch to say that the river was in his blood.

I'm sure he's not the only one. Throughout this land, rivers run through our lives. They are there in the names of cities, towns, villages and streets; they dictate how we navigate the land; and they can also flow within us, trickling down from ancestor to ancestor. Families, it seems, often cling to the rivers, especially before the link between livelihood and water was broken. The coracle-makers, like the Rogerses, the shipbuilders, the fishermen, the ferry men, the fowlers, the merchants, the millers and the mudlarks, the labourers and the lawless – all are part of the river's topography.

Some claim the river even shapes the temperament of those who live on or around it. The communities and families located upstream were once considered to be more thought-ful, more contemplative. The estuaries, in contrast, were more likely to breed people of speed and industry, of stealth and cunning. A populace that once treated the river as a god that needed appeasement and praise is acted upon, shaped by its wet fingers.

The Jackfield Rapids, the stretch of water I was warned about, isn't far downstream from Ironbridge. The nose of the canoe skips and bounces over the water as I approach, slapping the surface. I must have got the weight wrong when I reloaded. To the right there is a great hump of brown water, to the left a gentler sill from a line of rocks. I go left, gambling that the keel-less canoe will ghost over the submerged stone. Without James I find I'm talking to myself instead.

'Come on then, come on', a Delia Smith squawk of 'Let's be having you', and then I'm in. I paddle hard to the left, fear-ful that the Pipette won't respond, that she'll be sucked into the flow, to rotate and dump me out. But she answers the paddle, the bow twitching and jumping through troughs and swirls. She cuts clean through eddies and thin, brittle waves that snap into foam and roll into whirling balls that look like cocoa-dusted cappuccinos. The push from the rapids keeps the boat moving, past black rocks piled as a flood defence on the right, past flat, fat slabs the colour of damp cardboard to a slipway to a pub. I stop for breath, weighing up whether I should see if there are any beds available, but paddle on past the Coalport China Museum and the blackened bricks of its towering bottle kiln.

I'm glad to have finally left the town behind, and the houses that straggle after it. There is a loneliness to walking the streets alone that I don't feel on the river, surrounded by trees and rocks; that I certainly didn't feel on the Otter. It's a feeling that rasps and drags against walls and homes; it butts up and breathes sadly onto windowpanes and raps on doors. In towns and settlements, places where people come to group together for safety and trade, being alone is incongruous, it is to be an outsider. But here in the wooded sweep known as Apley Forge there is freedom again. It's just me and the canoe, carried and calmed by the water. The rain has eased with the lowering of the light and the woodland and river give off a scent of spring showers, a subtle perfume of leaf and rock.

I find my camp overlooking an island full of willow whips. The wood here is an old coppice that has drifted out of rotation. Straight poles of hazel and creamy ash rise from stools a good yard or so wide. The green, which drips with the memory of rain, is broken by a fizz of white elder and the baby-pink stars of campion. The river really does look like milk chocolate here. A Willy Wonka river, freshly mixed, aerated by the rapids upstream. Delicious.

When I wake it is dark. The birdsong and the wind have died away and the woodland is still. But I can hear a voice. Maybe two. A hushed conversation between friends. A low question and then a faster response; the tone rising and falling. I wonder who could be here at this time of night. Anglers perhaps? Gamekeepers coming back to claim their spot?

I peek through the screen of the trees. My fire has almost burnt out, leaving just a pile of red embers and tubes of black and white ash. My heart is beating faster. I can't see any torches or hear any movement. The low voice comes again, but this time the words end in wallowing, choking glug. It's not a human sound, but the voice of the Severn. This isn't the carefree chatter of a chalk stream or the song of an infant brook, but Sabrina's soulful record of her journey through gorges, towns and fields; of the civilisations she has seen rise and fall. It is a tale of the blood from their conflicts, the soot and ash of their ambitions; a roll-call of the weak and the unfortunate she has embraced as they fell into her cool waters.

It is an eternal voice. The human history of the Severn here may be one of attempts to exploit and conquer, of use and abuse, but the river, ever-lasting, has always pushed back, claiming lives and land. The forges, the quarries, the power stations and the age of industry have all been outlasted by the river, the one constant presence in this place, a continuous part of its identity. Perhaps it is this oldness, this sense of time that makes rivers such bewitching places. No wonder it sometimes feels as if rivers are more than just physical boundaries; they are a thin membrane between past and present, part of the character of the land.

The morning is clear, the sun lending the few discs of cloud hanging like UFOs over the hills a nectarine glow. The sky is light blue, washed out from yesterday's rain, but the river remains a silky chocolate-brown, tempered bright, glossy and slick by the new day. The paddling feels easy in water that is deep and darting.

Kingfishers dart overhead and a family of goosanders – necks stretched forward in effort – passes me on the other side of the river, travelling upstream. Behind the trees to the left I can see craggy rock faces of red sandstone, fractured by roots. Young willows look like they have fallen only to take root again, while stumps of grey wood cling to the lichen-frosted surface.

The wind begins to pick up as I near Bridgnorth. The rocks, now covered in steel cages like ugly hairnets to guard against landslides, slowly retreat behind the road. Ledges have been tacked on, shelves for the birds to fashion their nests in a place that has no doubt been their hunting ground for centuries. The sun lights a rippling path on the water. I can't help but feel a little bit haunted by last night. Not spooked but almost overwhelmed, as if I've got close to something bigger than me.

Bridgnorth is another place shaped by the physical path of the Severn; it cuts the place in two, separating Low Town from High Town. The town's very name comes from the crossing points that have stood here or hereabouts for more than a thousand years. Fording places often became towns, fortified and guarded, the river giving sustenance while also forming a defence. In its lower, estuarine reaches, where the Severn famously cleaves England from Wales, the Britons were said to have fled from the Saxons across its waters. Historians have suggested that the ways and beliefs of the Celts could have been protected by the moat of the river.

Perhaps it's not surprising that the river, which shapes the land and how we live, can also shape our cultures. Across the country, even the way we speak has been affected by the rivers' paths, forming communities of language as well as separating them. The Thames gave us Estuary English, a dialect that has spread like rising damp from the river valley across the south-east. A much maligned tide of wholly-holy; foot-strut and trap-bath splits. The glottal stop. The Stour, holding apart Suffolk and Essex, is a blue line between subtly different dialects. In Suffolk the rural accent is marked with its own peculiar glottal stops and yod-droppings that turn 'dew' to 'doo' and 'queue' to 'koo'. Across the river in Essex, the elongated vowels of Suffolk are clipped short ('sin' instead of 'seen').

Past Bridgnorth, with its busy streets and wide arched bridge, the river is full of current. My shoulders have been stiffened by fighting its pull and the wind that gusts from under clouds the colour of oily rags. I paddle on my knees past fields and caravan sites with perfectly tended gardens and empty fishing jetties to where the rocks rear up: a folding mass of reds, from new-brick to over-baked, sometimes lichen-white, sometimes lemon-sherbet.

I'd left the car four or five miles away from Bridgnorth at a caravan park that sweeps right down to the river, the only place I could see on the map for 20 miles where I wouldn't have to lug the canoe over the main road. But as soon as I arrive, it feels too soon. I don't feel ready to leave the river and the rocks; to stop being part of that cut into the earth.

Keen to stretch my legs before setting back off for Suffolk, I drive down to the Severn's banks at Blackstone Rock. I check a map in the car park and decide to take a short cut straight to the water rather than the path that winds through the Wyre Forest. But I've already lost my river legs and feel confused by the flow's direction; it seems to be going the wrong way. The road on the way here has cut out the meanders that swing the river round the compass.

I guess the waters of the Severn are famous for not doing what is expected. On about twenty-five days of the year, large surge waves travel as much as 18 miles up the river, reaching heights of 10 feet in the mid-stream and even more at the banks. The bore: a wave created by one of the highest tidal ranges in the world and a river that shallows and shrinks from five miles wide at Avonmouth to less than a hundred yards at Minsterworth.

There are sixty bores throughout the world. The Seine and Gironde in France both boast bores. In India there are the Indus, Hooghly and Brahmaputra; the Knik Arm in Alaska; the Petitcodiac in New Brunswick; the Amazon in Brazil and the biggest, with a spring tide wave of over 24 feet, the Ch'ient'ang'kian in China. In the UK there are eleven: on the Dee, the Eden, Great Ouse, Kent, Lune, Mersey, Nith, Parrett, Ribble, Trent and of course, the biggest and the second-largest in the world, on the Severn, which travels up to 13 miles per hour.

I slip off the walkway down a small muddy track that takes me to the water's edge. The Blackstone Rock, a great wedge of sandstone, rises sheer from the water. It is shrouded with trees, the water slapping against its exposed face. The Severn's bore, powerful though it is, doesn't reach this far inland, but this spot is still known for being a place of treacherous currents.

During the eighteenth century, hermits, perhaps holy men, used to live here, making use of the easily carved stone. Sailors would toss money and gifts from their trows (a type of cargo boat), hoping the prayers they received in return would be enough to ensure safe passage. According to legend the hermits would sometimes save children from drowning here, pulling them onto the safety of Blackstone Rock. Those who survived would take the Severn as their name. Another baptism: the river forever being part of their identity and their bloodline.

The river seems different to when I started my journey. The flow is still high, still fast, but my relationship to it has changed in some way. Even after a relatively short time on its waters, by understanding a bit more about its history, and that of the land surrounding it, I feel closer to it. I've begun to think that I take a piece of all the rivers I travel with me. They have all shaped me. Perhaps I've left a little piece of me out there too.

In this modern age the link between industry and water has been largely broken. Livelihood and life itself are no longer utterly dependent on the rivers' flows. But their waters still have a power over us, as they do the land. Having lived next to the Colne for so many years, it feels surprising to realise that being close to the river changes you.

CHAPTER 10

Into the wild

The sound of water is both everywhere and nowhere. A flat roar that shouts through the trees and rips the still of the early morning wide open. James and I are following a narrow path down to the river, stepping over raised roots, feet crunching on pine needles that scent the air. The torrent is visible now. A thundering deluge that slips and foams over granite rocks. A wooden bridge takes us to where the River Falloch bends and falls some 30 feet; a great fringe of peat-dyed water pouring over the glen, spat from the hill. It crashes and thunders down below; a river falling, the beauty and sublimity of a billion drops striking rock with the power of hammers. The pool beneath the falls has been cut and sculpted by the water into a smooth bowl. I can feel the spray on my face. After a night spent hunched up in the car it feels refreshing, a reward for the eight hours we spent driving through greasy sheets of rain yesterday. We've still got another three hours of travel ahead of us as we head towards our biggest trip yet: longer, further from home, a place where the water feels wilder.

Opposite the falls a viewing platform, woven out of steel rods oxidised brown from the perpetual mist, cantilevers out over the water. I clank out onto it. Cut into a front panel are words taken from Dorothy Wordsworth's diary in 1803 when she visited this spot with her brother William as part of their grand tour of Scotland. She too was struck by the sound of the waters that 'did not appear to come this way or that, from any particular quarter'. She writes how Samuel Taylor Coleridge told her that Glen-falloch means 'hidden vale', 'but William says, if we were to name it from our recollections of that time, we should call it the Vale of Awful Sound'.

The same year in which Dorothy Wordsworth sat by the Falloch Falls, an Act of Parliament authorised the construction of a giant canal to connect the west coast of Scotland at Corpach, near Fort William, with the east coast at Inverness. Running for 60 miles across the geological fault line of the Great Glen that forms the narrow neck of Scotland, the channel connects the wild, open waters of Loch Lochy, Loch Oich, Loch Ness and Loch Dochfour. The Great Glen Way, or rather the Great Glen Canoe Trail, also offers a chance for adventure: a rare chance to voyage across an entire country without having to leave your boat.

John MacGregor, the godfather of canoe exploration, suggested the trail would be a route worth exploring. At the end of *A Thousand Miles in the Rob Roy Canoe*, he said it could be possible to have a 'pleasant voyage' through the Kyles of Bute to Oban, before heading 'along the Caledonian Canal, until the voyager can get into the Tay for a swift run eastward'.

I'm keen to try. But the prevailing wind, which I've been told only changes direction for one week of the year, means such a route would be a slog even if we did have MacGregor's sail and his surly can-do attitude. Instead, we've decided to navigate west to east, hoping to reach the coast at Inverness in four days' time and eager to soak up the wild beauty of a route so much more remote than our previous voyages.

Despite our early rise, a combination of bad navigating by me and an overly officious lock-keeper means it is early afternoon when we finally get on the water. We put in the Pipe just after the system of locks at Banavie. Known as Neptune's Staircase, it is the longest staircase lock in Britain – lifting boats a total of 64 feet in the space of about 500 yards. More than a hundred masons worked for nearly four years to make the eight connected locks. It is an impressive piece of engineering.

The sun is out and strong, bouncing off greenish waters that shallow at the very sides to expose the canal's sloping stone walls. The banks are busy with other travellers, all heading east, a rag-tag caravan of explorers out for their own adventure.

The first leg of the journey is short, only about seven miles, taking us up to the mouth of the first stretch of open water, Loch Lochy. An easy first day. The towpaths are manicured neat, the kind of lawns you'd expect on a national monument, but fringed with clumps of gorse, their flowers butter-yellow, like the sun has been snagged on its thorns. There are blue-bells too. Long past in England, they are still in their prime here, frail bonnets nodding in the breeze. The seasons, it seems, do strange things in Scotland; spring and summer are slow to arrive but quick to leave. Behind it all is the Nevis Range, the dark flanks of the mountains rushing up into curdled lumps of low cloud.

Having the mountains around us is strange. The crags and fells are a complete contrast to the neatness of the canal. It is alien country: a different world to the arable sweeps of Suffolk and Essex, the embankments and townscapes of the Thames and the Cam. Even the red limestone of the Severn feels small in comparison. But it's hard to engage in the landscape, to escape the thought that it's all just some tableau, a mural that would rip and bulge if I could only get close enough to touch it. There seems to be a disconnect between land and water. The canal is too pedestrian, too meek against the wildness of the peaks. The feeling comes again as we pass a sluice from the River Lochy. The noise of the white water is overwhelming. The river, dashing its watery head against rocks, is wild and mad in comparison to the canal.

It only takes about an hour and a half to reach Gairlochy. Wild camping is forbidden along the banks of the canal so we have no choice but to make use of the informal site provided, set out on a patch of short grass between a lock bridge and the mouth of Loch Lochy. Half a dozen kayakers are already popping up pup tents and collecting wood for one of the fire pits. No doubt more will follow.

Close to my hammock is a small rowan tree. A mountain ash. According to folklore it is meant to keep away the evil eye. But it certainly doesn't keep off the midges. As the breeze drops, they arrive in billowing waves. I'm trying to eat, spooning soup under my head net with gloved hands. Each mouthful is a mission; one bite of mine means three of theirs. I soldier on but James has had enough. Suffering from tiredness and a headache, he gulps down his food and turns in before 8 p.m., swaddled in a mosquito net, his hat pulled down past his nose. He's snoring before I even have a chance to offer to tuck him in.

I'm tired too but I don't want to sleep. I feel too het up. The number of people at the campsite has grown dramatically and every spare patch of grass is covered. After the quietness and, in some cases, the solitude of the previous rivers and camping spots, I had thought that this trip – by far the most isolated – would be quieter still. In my head this one was just us. After driving the length of the country to get away, I feel the need to escape more than ever.

I decide to go for a walk. I cross over the lock to the east bank and stroll back the way we paddled; the bay, boats and the whitewashed walls of the toilet block behind me. The sun is still bright – this far north it won't set until much later – but its rays only penetrate the canal's edges, turning the quarried stone bricks to glowing gold, while in the centre of the channel the water stays glossy black. Aubergine and oil, shifting, glinting and very, very deep. Beyond the canal the clouds have finally lifted from Ben Nevis, exposing its ramp-like south face and chewed crags. It is elephantine in profile. Patches of old snow are packed into crevices and gullies like swirls on a Rorschach test.

Laughter carries on the wind as I walk back to our hammocks. Looking around this campsite, and after the calm, genteel canal route, I'm worried that the trail is a bit busy and too well trodden. So many people, flushing toilets, washing machines, tumble driers and showers – it all jars with that lofty conceit of having an authentic adventure. Yet I also know that every river I have experienced over the last year has been an adventure in ways I really couldn't have predicted: the dunking in the upper Thames; the eyots of the lower; the ice of the Lark; the sleekness of the beaver.

I came here to find a sense of wildness on a scale not possible in the lowland of England and, away from this canal, in lochs with water deep enough to swallow entire villages, it's possible I might yet do so. But I'm also sure there'll be other things, moments that rise to the surface like a jellyfish mooning out of the depths, that will bind me to this place; that will leave its mark on me as water does on stone.

From the mouth of the canal the loch curves round to the north, to form a large bay cloaked with dense pine that spreads from the water's edge and up the grey sides of the mountains. The south bank is closer, again deeply wooded; the mountains dip and swoop along the loch's steep, forested sides. I feel a shiver up my back; a sense of appreciation, not so much of the human effort that connected canal to loch, but at the experience of floating above a fault line, of navigating 700 million years of the earth's history. The Great Glen Geological Fault extends from coast to coast. It is still active; between 1768 and 1906 there were fifty-six earthquakes recorded in the vicinity of the Great Glen, with the last big tremor recorded near Inverness in 1934. In 2013 a quake with a magnitude of 2.4 on the Richter Scale hit over a mile beneath Drumnadrochit, near Loch Ness. People as far away as Inverness reported movement and some described hearing a 'roaring sound'. The *Daily Mail* blamed it on Nessie.

Navigating Lochy now, you'd be forgiven for thinking that the glacier that once filled this rift during the last Great Ice Age had only just retreated. There is an untampered-with oldness that I didn't expect to see outside of the wilds of Canada or Alaska. It is both stark and beautiful. The water and land combine in a shifting palette of greys, blacks and greens. Grey on the mountain, the sky, the tree trunks crystallised with silver lichen and on the rocks licked wet by the water. Green in the pines and the great puddings of moss that slip towards the loch's edge. Black in the water itself, like squid ink or starless space.

We had intended to follow the shoreline, but the canal entrance lines us up with the end of the bay, a headland about a mile away, perhaps more. We set off, the wind rising and blowing against us as we head for the horizon, the sky meeting the water in the narrowest of mountain passes. The waves are bigger than I expected and faster. As we ride over one and into its trough, another one hits. The Pipe cuts through to leave a sheet of water that slides over her nose and into James's lap.

With so much water, so much landscape, it's hard to gain perspective or gauge our speed. The single white house that clings to the loch's edge by the mouth of the bay gets neither closer nor further away. The waves, once black messy humps, folding over themselves with a white-spittle foam, driven by the wind become black horses' heads. They gallop towards us with bubbling manes, tossing and bouncing us from their liquid flanks. They break without warning too, exploding underneath us or collapsing meekly as we get ready to ride them. Up and down, lifted and dropped. I'm quite surprised I don't feel sick; maybe I have finally found my sea legs in the centre of Scotland.

Loch Lochy is said to mean Loch of the Dark Goddess. According to legend it is home to a kelpie, a river horse that crept from the lake and assumed an equine shape to graze on the shore. Known here as Lord of the Lake or the Water King, when disturbed he would plunge back into the water. His power was said to be so great that he could shake the universe, his movements being both awesome and destructive, overturning boats and enticing mares and children to their deaths. Perhaps it is he, not the fault line, which caused the towns around the Great Glens to shake.

There's no let up on the loch – there can't be if we want to keep going forward. Our rhythm is steady enough. Finally, after an hour, maybe two, the whole waterscape shifts. The beach, the rocks, the spindle sharp pines appear to change position suddenly, as if we have been paddling with a hand over one eye. Now we're within touching distance of the shore and we follow its curve, exposing the canoe's sides to the waves as we paddle a hundred yards further to a beach that had glowed yellow from out on the loch. Large spits have formed a cove, a crescent created by the suck and scour of windswept water. I had expected sand, but the shore is made up of honey-coloured gravel, studded with rock and larger stone.

We beach the Pipe and look back. The mouth of the canal has been swallowed up in the distance, its half-a-mile-wide opening unidentifiable against wood and mountain. James flops down on the stones and I join him, lying on my back looking over the gravel spit and on towards where we are heading, where the water is funnelled through the wide, knobbly V of the mountains. After yesterday's tensions, I think we're both feeling happier. Less tired, less harried by people. It feels stupid, arrogant even, to have expected to have the entire route across Scotland to ourselves: to have been momentarily disappointed that this trek, this secret window, had already been discovered and opened by someone else. Yet now that we are on our own the landscape does feel different. I've always thought the idea of wilderness was just that: an idea. The landscape is always farmed, tarmacked, developed or managed. There is also the sense that every wilderness is destroyed as soon as its light hits the back of the human eye, the landscape turned cultural by just our presence. An encounter with pristine wilderness and the untouched is always, necessarily, out of our reach. But sitting here now, it feels that even if this place is not pristine and undisturbed, it is at least wild in a very raw and visceral sense.

The wind is dying down as we push out round the gravel spit and back onto the loch. It's a dreamy paddle. Conversation-free, just dip and pull, the odd glug from the Pipe as she turns into a small wave or the gentle trickle of water slipping under our keel. A dipper flits from boulder to boulder, lowering itself to the water as if weak at the knees.

The end of the loch at South Laggan is busy, though, full of cruisers, kayaks, barges and sailing dinghies. The campsite is small and meagre-looking too, and neither of us is keen to repeat the experience of last night; we want somewhere a bit more remote, somewhere it feels like we are in Scotland. We didn't come this far to make do with a postage stamp of grass. Instead, we carry on east.

After the wide wildness of Lochy I hadn't been looking forward to being back on the canal. Hemmed in, the water itself feels almost lifeless. The sides are as golf-green neat as Banavie but at least there are pines here, crowding down to the water's edge, scenting the air with the cool smell of rushing sap. The rain, long expected, has arrived, soft and drizzly, forming shining beads of mist on our hats. This stretch has felt like a hard slog and my mood doesn't improve much at Loch Oich. The loch feels narrow and wooded, with scattered buoys in fading greens and pinks. There are signs hammered into the islands and banks. Private, no fishing. There is a gloominess to this place that comes from the rain, the closeness to the banks and the dark trees.

We stop to stretch our legs. As we wander down to the local shop we spot an obelisk set into the curve of the roadside wall, its peak topped with a stone ball. Except, getting closer, I realise it's not a ball at all but a hand, clutching a dagger and grasping the hair of seven decapitated heads, their sightless eyes staring at the black waters of Oich. It is a monument to a *Game of Thrones*-style bloodletting. Hot vengeance dressed up as cool justice.

The story goes that in September 1663 Alexander, the chief of the Keppoch family and a member of the powerful MacDonald clan, attended a party with his brother Ranald following their return from school in France. A fight broke out with their cousins, perhaps because they mocked the European twang to their accent and new love of French customs. Or maybe it was more calculated: an attempt to overthrow a clan chief. Either way, both men were killed that night. Iain Lom, known as Bald Iain, then the Poet Laureate of Scotland, called for revenge for his kinsmen. Iain was put in charge of a group of fifty men who travelled to where the seven killers – Alexander MacDonald (one of the victims' namesake) and his six sons – lived. They arrived to find the house in Inverlair barricaded, so set it on fire, killing all those inside. Their heads were cleaved from their charred bodies and carried by the bard to the waters of Loch Oich, where he washed them in a well before sending them on to the gallows of Edinburgh. The monument was erected much later by the then chief of Clan MacDonald in 1812.

James's headache has returned and he's keen to stop for the night. But I'm determined to go further, to get closer to Loch Ness. I can feel it, taste it. There's something magnetic about being so close to so much wild water. The light softens but doesn't fail as we pass through the next weir and loch gates. The River Oich runs alongside us as we paddle, a wild siren song to the silence of our man-made waterway.

Our campsite, when we find it some five or six miles west of Fort Augustus, is otherworldly. The trees, a mix of birch and alder, give way to swamp dotted with scrub and thorns, beyond which pine stand close-knit and dark. A faint trail, made by horses, leads through the camp and up the bank. Their droppings are the driest thing here. It's hard to find somewhere that will support the hammocks. The trees look healthy enough, hugged and bearded by moss. But almost everything we touch comes away in our hands. The perpetual damp of the Highlands has turned birch to sponge. The wood on the ground is rotten too, falling into wet splinters with the tread of our boots. Moss covers everything. Rocks, fallen trees are all blanketed in the stuff, sometimes in layers almost a foot thick. It's a woodland of fairy tales and horror movies. I can imagine the moss moving in overnight, sprawling over the hammocks and creeping over our sleeping faces, the only evidence of our passing being a canoe-shaped mound.

I shudder and slap my wrists. The midges hang in the air in dense clouds. I have a head net on but they still find a way in. My hands and lower arms, still uncovered, are dark with them – a living, biting sleeve. They don't seem to like tattoos, though, chewing into the veins of my hand and the ink-free patches on my arms. We have bought joss sticks and citronella candles, but it's little more than mood-lighting for the midges' supper. Their constant attention is maddening. 'God, I just want to rip my own face off,' James says.

I realise the back of my neck is still exposed and run my hand down it; it comes away sooty from crushed midge, the lumps already hardening and itching. My hairline and eyelids are all throbbing and one bite is coming up on the side of my neck, the skin tight, knotted like a bubo.

I sleep fitfully, dreaming of dark water and creeping moss sliding over my legs and up to my groin. I wake with the first light and run my hands over my head and face, feeling the Braille map of midge feeding spots and blood-letting. Bumps on bumps on bumps. I must look a state. I feel OK though, excited about the day ahead and the prospect of Loch Ness.

James calls from his hammock. He wants to know if I heard the horse. Sometime in the middle of the night it had walked through the camp and spent an hour with its nose pressed up to James's tarp, exhaling with loose-lipped consternation. 'I was scared stiff,' he says. 'I wanted to ask you what I should do but I didn't want to make a noise.'

It seems the horse wasn't the only night-time visitor. Great armies of slugs cover everything. They have slid into bags, cooking pots, boots, and cover the bottom of the canoe with a snotty map of their movements. We flick them from the outside of our drysuits and zip up. James freezes as he bends his arms and legs to squeeze out the last of the air from his suit. He shudders and mock-gags before unzipping himself again. A slug, black as liquorice, thick as a thumb, is squished into his arm.

The woman behind the counter at Fort Augustus's pharmacy is adamant.

'Oh no,' she says, 'we don't have nae midges here, just Nessies.'

She hands over the bite cream with a smile and the old boy behind me joins in.

'Aye she's right laddie, just Nessies and tourists.'

I grab two coffees from a neighbouring cafe and walk across the bridge over the River Oich, the water below churning brown and cream against rocks. The man in the pharmacy wasn't wrong about the tourists. The town is full of them, patrolling the streets with selfie sticks, filing into cafes and gift shops and milling at the foot of the staircase lock that cuts the town in two and raises and lowers boats 40 feet from the canal to Loch Ness. Earlier, as we took a breather from lugging the Pipe the 200-yard route from the first lock to the last, a few people had asked to touch her or take pictures, with one even standing inside making victory signs. To be honest, after the wildness of the loch and the strange isolation of our campsite, it was something of a shock suddenly to be confronted with civilisation. It felt like we'd been out on our own for much longer than a day.

James has been busy reorganising the canoe, making sure we've got all the essentials to hand. We chat and make jokes as we drink our coffee but there is a tension too. We both know this is serious now. Loch Ness is a proper piece of water. In fact, there is more water in Loch Ness than all the other lakes in England, Scotland and Wales put together. Some 22½ miles long and between one and 1½ miles wide, the depth runs to 754 feet – deep enough to sink the Empire State Building. The loch is said to be big enough to hold the world's population ten times over.

Behind us the cloud is low. It cuts the mountains in half, rolling down steep, wooded sides like steam, or a slow-motion eruption, pouring towards the loch and the town. A cloud sea with the tide coming in. The loch seems empty of boats and I'm not sure whether to be pleased that we will have the water to ourselves – that we won't have to contend with the wake from speedboats and pleasure cruisers – or worried that they know something we don't. We've been advised to pick a side and stick to it. Crossing the loch is meant to be avoided, perhaps because of the traffic on the water, but also because it means being broadside to the waves.

The canal's mouth widens out onto the loch and we head for the slope of the south bank. The water is calm, with just a gentle swell nudging us along. The enormity of the loch is breathtaking. The black water is framed by rolling hills and pines to the north and mountain ash to our right. Closer to the bank we can see there is no way we can really pull in if it gets rough. Crags and overhangs have sent lumps of gran-ite crashing to the foreshore, where they have whitened with lichen that forms in bird-shit splodges. From the splits and ledges trees still grow, their roots scrabbling into the splits and cracks in the rock, the wind turning them into Highland bonsais. Occasionally landslips have wiped away and scrubbed up trees, leaving a scree slope of grey and white.

The wind is already gusting. Unlike on Lochy, it is at our backs, and the water is choppy; the swell picking us up and putting us down again, pushing us forward like a parent at a playground swing. We've never had the waves behind us like this before and it is slightly disconcerting; I end up keeping an eye on the black waves that chase after us, making sure the canoe is properly placed. It's an odd sensation being lifted above James too; hurried along in the air until the wave passes to the front and it's James's turn to climb – paddle held above his head, instinctively rising from his seat with the motion. The waves aren't directly behind us, though. Instead they flow north-east, which means that to keep from hitting the bank we have to tack out into the loch and then turn back towards the shore between waves.

We take a break on a gravel beach, and by the time we set off again it looks like the weather is starting to turn. The forecast today is not great. After a week of Scottish sun, normal service is due to be resumed with rain and wind. From time spent in the Highlands, I know that whole seasons can play out in a single day: rain and snow, making way for sun. But on the loch the changes are even more extreme. The sweeping patches of blue that we have been heading for have slowly been eaten up by ominous-looking clouds that have rolled off the mountains. Although we are still paddling in the sun, across the other side of the loch, perhaps a mile away, maybe less, maybe more, I can see curtains of rain driving with the south-westerly wind: the drops shiver like minnows in a stream, the clouds forming dark halos round the brown tips of the mountains.

Just a small amount of rain on Loch Ness can make a big difference. The loch is fed by seven major rivers: the Oich, Tarff, Enrick, Coiltie, Moriston, Foyers and Farigaig, plus numerous burns. The catchment for Loch Ness is so large that just a quarter of an inch of rain can add 11 million tonnes of water to the loch. It has been known for the loch to rise by seven feet in downpours, and I've heard a two-foot shift is common.

The waves are definitely getting bigger. We bump up and over them, hitting them square on before steering hard in their trough, putting them behind us again. Perhaps we shouldn't have stopped; we should have made hay while the sun shone. While I was looking at the Well of Seven Heads yesterday James had got chatting to a woman in one of the large white leisure cruisers. She said they had been warned off Loch Ness as they approached from Dochgarroch. But, knowing she would probably never return, they sailed on. The four-foot waves smashed glasses and bounced the fruit bowl off the ceiling.

The water feels different now. With the increased cloud and the first spots of rain hitting us, the loch seems more austere, less accommodating. Truly wild. The black waves are no longer a thing of sun-gilded fascination but an inky threat. The water gets rougher more quickly than I thought possible, the one-foot waves growing to three feet, and it becomes harder to change direction, to turn in the swell. One, then two waves slop over the Pipe's side. The water, so dark that I'm constantly surprised to see my paddle, is perfectly clear as it swills about in the bottom of the canoe. But more water is coming in, glugging over the gunwales and landing in our laps.

James shouts over his shoulder. 'Do you think we should head to the shore?'

I look to the side of me at another wave that chases along the edge of the canoe before almost turning to dump more water inside.

'Yeah, we're getting swamped'.

I lean into the paddle, spinning the Pipe towards the bank, the waves helping; picking us up and putting us close, perhaps too close, to rocks that submerge and surface again with streaming, foaming heads. It feels as if the world is tilting forward and back, sloshing the loch further up the banks. I can't see in front but James shouts directions past granite shards and hidden rocks.

'Hard right. Left. Right. Right.'

If we hit a rock now I know we would spin and, with our vulnerable broadside exposed to the pushing water, we would surely go over. Worse still, it would probably smash the boat to pieces. We keep going, gritting our teeth and bracing our legs against the insides of the canoe, while James scans the shore for a break in the rocks that would allow us to land. There's a low, scraping moan as the Pipe drags over a submerged lip of rock and pitches; I hold my breath, leaning and paddling hard to get free. My stomach flips, my heart is thumping out of my chest. James shouts out more directions. We have to keep moving.

There is a small cove ahead, and although it is facing the waves and will provide little shelter from the wind, the beach looks clear of large rocks. We line up with the gap in the rocks and start to paddle hard, the canoe's movements sluggish from the water inside her that cannons from end to end in the swell. But the waves give us a final shove, sending the Pipe juddering over stones that are just under the surface and onto the beach. She sheds paint but stays intact. We're home and almost dry.

We're happy to be safe but there is a thrill too from the experience, an adrenaline buzz that makes the heart race as much as the mountains and water had once quietened them. But now we're on dry ground the thin line between success and abject bloody failure is also clearer. While the rest of the shore along Ness looked untouched, apart from maybe the odd burnt log, here the beach and rocks are littered with shards of plastic, the remains of a smashed boat that lies upended further up, almost hidden in the scrub. The hull has been cracked in two, a tale of rough weather and a less successful landing.

I can't quite believe how quickly the weather changed. Like the flick of a switch on a swimming pool's wave machine. The loch as far as I can see is in turmoil, black ridges that rush to the sides, collapsing in their speed or tripping up on rocks littering the edges. The movement of the humped water is mesmerising and strangely animal. Monstrous, even. The myth of Nessie makes sense.

Ever since St Columba confronted what his cousin, Vita Columbae, Adomnán of Iona, described as a great 'water beast' in 565 there have been reports of a giant creature lurking in Loch Ness. Tales from the banks, the roadside and the water itself describe, variously, a creature with the appearance of an upturned boat; a 'huge snail with a long neck'; something 'salamander-like'; a large animal with a horse-like mane; a beast with an eel-like head; a giant pig; a hairy hippo; a monster with huge flippers. According to Gary Campbell, Registrar of Sightings for Loch Ness, there have been 1,087 sightings recorded to date, with eight taking place in 2016.

Some of the reports and the famous photographic 'proofs' are clearly hoaxes. But what's interesting about many of the eyewitness accounts is that they were (and still are) made by apparently level-headed people: doctors, police officers, school teachers have all reported seeing Nessie rising from the black waters of the loch. Yet no trace of the beast has ever been found. Monster hunters, submarines, scientists with sonar have all drawn a blank – or at least produced nothing that cannot be explained by way of otters, seals, boat wakes, swimming deer, floating logs and underwater waves.

I don't believe for a minute there is a monster here. But I can understand why its lure has captivated so many people, drawn them in like a kelpie. I feel like I've sensed something similar: an old, odd and almost overwhelming power in the waters of the loch that, especially when the weather turns, can feel . . . well, more than natural. But there is something else too. In a country shorn of its megafauna, the idea that some ancient, mysterious predator may still survive in the dark depths is as tantalising and appealing as it is fantastical.

Having waited out the storm, the rest of the day is stop-start, paddling in lulls and resting during squalls as far as Foyers, about halfway up Loch Ness. There are no boats, even smashed ones, to be seen. The odd cruiser and the inflatable boat that bounced passengers up and down the loch this morning have all gone, maybe victims of the weather, or perhaps they just don't go this far. We're protected, though, from the worst of the weather by the shape of the loch, with the south bank curving round to the south east. This part of Ness is calm enough to keep going even when the wind bullies the water further out back into lolloping waves.

We finally stop just in sight of Urquhart Castle, on a stretch of gravel and stone that is almost white in the sun. The foreshore is sheltered and dotted with trees, alder, birch and hazel, with a view over the loch to the castle, a reddish block on the waterline of the north coast.

It is easily the best camp we have struck. The hammocks are strung from neighbouring trees, next to a small, flat rock that is perfect for the stove and a larger rock that we can use as a card table. The wind is still strong: enough to keep the midges off, but light enough not to chill. The water, shallow around the bay, reflects a sky that is now almost free of cloud.

We're both in good spirits and, while the kettle boils, go for a swim. I splash out as far as I dare, watching the bottom turn from sun-warmed gold to peaty black. The swell on the loch has dropped, and as I lie on my back the waves no longer feel hostile and frightening but caressing: gentle hands that carry me back to the shore. I flip and breast-stroke out to where the sun has lit a path through the mountains and then hang there, treading cold, black water. I can feel the chill but it doesn't bother me. After a day spent trying to stay in the canoe it's good to celebrate by abandoning it, to slip from a wooden skin back into my own. To be immersed in it all. Landscapes and waterscapes require participation; when you are in the water there is no scenery: limbs and loch merge.

We return to the shore and place large stones in a circle in between the flat rocks of our camp and start a fire, the dead wood blazing in seconds. We warm Ness-chilled hands and arrange our boots to steam dry. Neither of us is in a hurry to turn in tonight. Instead we stay up with the sun, talking and joking; scrabbling in our packs for more supplies, more rum, more gin. Darkness never really falls. The polar summer smokes away to a ghostly twilight; the moon a waxing wedge over the water, the shore milk-soaked and silver.

It is already light when I get up to retie my hammock, which has somehow slipped down the tree to deposit me on the gravel. I check my watch, it's 3 a.m. I decide to walk down to the shore and sit on one of the rounded stones by the water's edge, my body still warm from my sleeping bag, my head fuzzy with sleep. The night is calm, the water lapping a lullaby. I would happily stay here a long time. I want to make the most of it before this last wild, secret window closes.

It feels like a long paddle to reach Clansman Harbour – where tourists line up for boat tours – and towards Lochend. We cling to the north bank, feeling the wildness draining away with the rumble and clatter of the A82 rushing towards Inverness. It's not just the noise; the surroundings have changed too: they have become more human. Two more dippers hop along the edges, but rocks are not their only perches. Entire cars, perhaps from crashes decades ago, have toppled onto the foreshore, twisted and brown, their chassis long departed to leave them crouched and beetle-like, engines exposed. They are joined by armchairs, sofas and an entire three-piece suite, all pushed over the stony roadside ledge to upend and roll towards the loch. Snared in branches, knitted in scrub, they sit unclaimed alongside lorry tyres, ladders and a fridge with its door swung open into a rust-locked wave.

Ness gradually narrows to meet Loch Dochfour and then it's just a short paddle to Dochgarroch and the final stretch of the canal. The landscape transforms from meadows, farms and countryside into suburban edgelands and then city, the grey of rock making way for grey concrete. The outskirts of Inverness. We haven't spoken much since we left Ness. Both of us are tired and sad that the last of the wild water is behind us. I feel annoyed with myself too. The River Ness is nearby, I can hear it, and part of me regrets the decision we made at Loch Dochfour to stick to the canal. Practical rather than adventurous, I was too worried about ending up somewhere I could get a cab back to the car.

We press on, testing our speed: past the rowing club; under bridges and through open lock gates; past teenagers swan-diving and cat-calling, smoking and lounging on the banks; past families walking, anglers and bike riders, to reach an end that we didn't want to come. Muirhead. Next stop the sea. We're finally out of land.

The next morning we plan to get up early and hit the road, but it's hard to leave our guest-house beds, hammering the sleep button on our phones' alarms and drifting off again. I'm happy to be heading home but I just can't get the memory of the Loch Ness camp out of my head. It was a time when it felt like we had found the journey we were hoping for; as if that landlocked water was always ours to find. Every portage and muddy bank, every insect bite, bruise and blister, every mislaid piece of kit, impromptu dunking, every frozen bone and burnt piece of skin had been connected to that moment.

After breakfast, I shower and inspect the few bites that are still raised on my face. I'd realised last night that it's almost a year to the day that we first launched the Pipe. I never expected to have come so far, to have had so much fun. A lot has changed. I can see on the misted glass of the bathroom mirror that I have new lines on my forehead. I lean closer, pulling and pushing skin tanned from days on the water. My hands are calloused and roughened. I wear the river on my fingers and in my shoulders and in my chest, which has broadened and stiffened.

I feel different too. The way I view the landscape, the way I experience it has changed, shifted on its axis. To journey through rivers and waterways is also to reclaim them. Rights to walk and roam over land have been hard won and fiercely protected. A similar defence of paddling is needed. Perhaps these journeys can be a part of that. An inspiration for others to dip their blades; to feel the river's pull.

I've always felt that I've been on the borders with nature. I've wandered in and out. It is a relationship I have cherished but rarely developed, like a good friend you only see at Christmas and funerals. The rivers and the wild water of the lochs, though, have allowed something longer, deeper, all-encompassing: joy, wonder and in some cases even flickers of life-affirming terror. I feel like I've shed the rust gathered from being landlocked and lazy. The habits and responsibilities of modern life can be hard to shake off, the white noise difficult to muffle. But the water has returned me to my senses. I've been reborn in a baptism of the Waveney, Stour, Lark, Thames, Cam, Colne, Wye, Otter, Severn and Ness. The river leaves its mark on us, long after we've returned to land: we are never quite the same, changed by an experience that has flooded into our lives. It gives new meaning to the hearthside when we return.

Yet I still don't think of myself as a canoeist. My paddling feels more like how Henry David Thoreau described walking. Perhaps I am a walker on water. A floating flâneur, setting out 'in the spirit of undying adventure, never to return, prepared to send back our embalmed hearts only as relics to our desolate kingdoms'. But of course we always do return.

I can hear James knocking about in the room, packing his gear and snapping on the TV to listen to the news. He's dressed and raring to go. I can't help but feel intensely fond of him. There's a pang of sadness too that this is the last trip. Our last feckless outing. I owe him a lot, not just on these trips but for building the Pipe, the wooden foundations of our friendship, in the first place: a bond, birthed from water and hopefully as enduring.

The drive back home is long and tiring, the rain falling in sheets that slow traffic to a crawl and hide the mountains. I stop for nearly every river. Findhorn, Dulnain, Allt na Criche, Allt Criochaidh, Allt Coire Chleirich, the Spey, the Truim, River Garry (now fully fledged and roaring, carrying the taste of Ness) the Tummel (twice), Tay, the Earn, the River Forth, Clyde, Annan, Esk, Eden and others whose names I could not see, all rolling off the land to the sea. I want to travel each and every one of them. I feel the same sense of excitement that I did when we first set out.

Near the border with England some stones from Ness that I had forgotten I'd stowed in the canoe tumble onto the windscreen with a sickening crack. I pull over and check for damage while James rocks the car as he checks the ratchets holding the Pipe on the roof rack.

I shout to him over the traffic, waving to get his attention.

'You know this isn't the end,' I say. 'We should just think of this as a long portage.'

Acknowledgements

I am hugely in debt to a number of people who made this book possible.

First, thank you to James Treadaway, for building the good ship Pipe and for being its uncomplaining engine throughout. No words can convey how grateful to him I am and how much I treasure his friendship.

A huge thank you also goes to Jennie Condell, Pippa Crane and the rest of the team at Elliott & Thompson who have been unfailingly supportive and believed in me enough to give me this opportunity. Thanks to Melissa Harrison for her kind words of advice and for including me in the wonderful seasonal anthology she edited for E&T that started it all.

I am also hugely grateful to Isabel Vogel for her readings of early forms of this book. Her sensitive, thoughtful and insightful suggestions were utterly invaluable.

I would like to thank Julian Roughton and Simone Bullion, who generously checked the accuracy of some of the wildlife passages (any remaining mistakes about flora and fauna are, sadly, mine and mine alone). Thanks too go to Shaun Norris,

Mike Andrews, Hawk Honey, Emma Keeble, Will Cranstoun, Joe Bell-Tye and Sophie Mayes and the rest of the lovely team at Lackford Lakes for allowing me to work in their office; and thank you to Suffolk Wildlife Trust (particularly Kerry Stranix and Christine Luxton) for giving me the time to write up.

There have been a number of people that have been generous with their time while I was working on this book, so thank you to: Devon Wildlife Trust, specifically Mark Elliott for his time in explaining the beaver projects; Douglas Caffyn; Keith Day from River Access for All; Ruth Norfolk and Richard Atkinson from British Canoeing; Mark Lloyd from The Angling Trust; Chris Coode of Thames21; Nathalie Cohen of the Thames Discovery Programme; and the Royal Canoe Club in Teddington for their hospitality.

I would also like to thank everyone who has offered kind words and encouragement from the river bank, particularly Rob and his family, whose walk along the Thames we spectacularly ruined, but who still made sure we were safe and warm. I hope one day to be able to thank you properly.

Thanks also to Mark Ereira-Guyer and Simon Wallace for canoe advice during the early stages and to my dad Phil and Anna Bird, who both provided taxi services to and from some of the local rivers.

Finally, I would like to thank my friends and family, especially Jen, Seth and Eliza, for their love, almost limitless patience and understanding. They are my paddles and my anchor.

Index